THE SUCCESS ZONES
Desire . Align . Manifest.

Guide and Workbook

By Dr. Theresa L. Smith, D.C.

THE SUCCESS ZONES
Desire. Align. Manifest.

By Dr. Theresa L. Smith, D.C.

ISBN Paperback: 979-8-9992516-0-2
ISBN Ebook/Digital: 979-8-9992516-1-9

Table of Contents

INTRODUCTION 7

CHAPTER 1

THE MIND 11

CHAPTER 2

GOOD CHOICES VS. ALIGNED CHOICES 30

CHAPTER 3

HEART-GUIDED WRITING 39

CHAPTER 4

YOUR SHADOW 41

CHAPTER 5

ALIGN ALL ENERGIES WITHIN 44

CHAPTER 6

MANIFESTATION 48

CHAPTER 7

INTUITION 51

CHAPTER 8

CLARITY PROCESS 54

CHAPTER 9

PUTTING IT ALL TOGETHER 57

THE SUCCESS ZONES WORKBOOK

CHAPTER 1

YOUR MIND WORKSHEETS 62

CHAPTER 2

GOOD CHOICES VS. ALIGNED CHOICES WORKSHEETS
. . . . 70

CHAPTER 3

HEART -GUIDED WRITING WORKSHEETS 76

CHAPTER 4

YOUR SHADOW WORKSHEETS. 81

CHAPTER 5

ALIGN ALL ENERGIES WITHIN WORKSHEETS 85

CHAPTER 6

MANIFESTATION WORKSHEETS 92

CHAPTER 7

INTUITION WORKSHEETS 98

CHAPTER 8

CLARITY WORKSHEETS 102

CHAPTER 9

PUTTING IT ALL TOGETHER WORKSHEETS 108

THE SUCCESS ZONES
Desire . Align . Manifest.

INTRODUCTION

I was already successful as a chiropractor and entrepreneur, but something wasn't adding up.

I was working hard, helping people, doing everything "right" — yet I wasn't making the kind of money I knew I was capable of.

I made just enough to survive, but never more. No matter what I did, true abundance remained elusive.

And then, something happened that completely shattered my perspective.

I had been taught that we create everything that happens in our lives, but after a vicious attack on my body and brain, I couldn't reconcile this belief anymore. Did I really create this? If so, why?

At the same time, I learned a shocking truth: 95% of dis-ease is caused by what we think and feel. This changed everything for me.

It made me question my entire role as a chiropractor. I was adjusting people's bodies, but their real problems were in their thoughts, emotions, and subconscious programming.

So, I went searching.

I studied dozens of different modalities, mindsets, and transformational practices. I tried everything. And after years of learning, testing, and refining, I discovered something profound:

√ It's **NOT** about clearing every belief you've ever had. (That's an impossible battle.)

√ It's **NOT** about working harder or trying to change who you are.

√   **IT IS ABOUT** knowing how to direct your mind, listen to your soul, and take aligned action.

That's exactly what I share in this book.

Now, in my life, I don't push. I don't force. I don't struggle. I am present, focused, and aligned. I know how to adapt, transform, and transition—anytime, anywhere.

And I want to show you how to do the same.

This book has the real "how-to" for success, manifestation, and alignment. It's not woo-woo or wishful thinking. It's a logical, structured approach rooted in science, the subconscious mind, and the power of imagination.

When you complete this book, you will always know exactly what to do and how to do it to achieve your desires. No doubts. No worries. Just clarity, alignment, and results.

It is simply using these tools and loving yourself enough to choose YOU.

While the book appears to be relatively small, it is filled with the information and tools that I use to live my life and ensure I always achieve my desires.

I have spent thousands of hours and as much, if not more, money to glean this information.

What seemed to be the most important tools to use were ways to think and manifest my deepest heart's desires.

With that comes knowing that I will always have my desires, and that brings me peace.

I need the wisdom to listen to myself and accept all of me because none of us can fix ourselves enough to ever get our heart's desires.

It is only by focusing on our desires, listening to our heart, feeling what it feels like to have it, being, and doing that works, and understanding how the mind works so that we can direct it, learning about how you operate, accepting it, loving ourselves anyway.

Following our intuition and our heart, using heart-guided writing to share our soul's desires, are all specific ways to get our desires.

I am sharing the specifics, the ways to really learn what is in your heart and bring it forth. I got tired of all the fluff that never led to anything except back to where I started.

In my opinion, the tools shared within these pages are the only ones necessary to achieve your heart's desire.

There are silent and invisible instructions that are always being heard by all of your parts. When you say you are going to do something and don't, what message are you telling yourself? What instructions do you receive?

Our human journey starts with a goal, which creates a tensional structure; all of your mind wants to seek resolution and will pull the goal toward you.

Learning how to focus and choose from the heart will always bring your desired goal into reality.

Also, have you ever noticed people saying things like, "So and so is a pain in my butt."

Do not put emotions into the body, do not say these things like "this is killing me." Because you hear this, every cell in your body hears it and follows the directions.

This is why people have a hunchback, or kyphosis; their bodies are protecting their hearts.

Posture is a huge key as to what is going on emotionally.

When the truth is uncomfortable, it is because of the meaning you put on it. It doesn't mean anything unless you believe it means something; it doesn't. Use it as fuel to create a difference. Just notice what meaning you put on it. Then decide if that is really true, decide if that is all there is, decide if that is where you are going to stay stuck.

That which you resist persists. This means that if you consistently resist parts of you, they will persist and continuously take you back to where you started. This pertains to anything you resist. You cannot have what you desire when your beliefs are running the show. Use your will to let go of conditions of creating. Engage the genius of what you love, be, do, and have to create.

The end result engages your natural abilities, your genius. You just may not recognize it yet.

When we choose to act on our heart's desires, we are using our will, which leads to success. We can choose to fix ourselves or focus on our desires. It is that simple. Unless you say it's hard, then I believe you.

After absorbing what this book holds, you will be able to recognize how you operate and decide to choose your power. You will always be able to get what you desire using all the tools in this book.

If you do need assistance, and to find the meditations, go to **https://www.thesuccesszones.com**. There are different programs available

With all the love in my heart and beyond, enjoy!

Dr. Theresa

CHAPTER 1

THE MIND

Your Mind Is Powerful—But Who's in Control?

Our mind is incredibly powerful, with multiple parts that serve different roles. When we understand how these parts work together, we can learn how to manipulate and rewire our own brain to function in alignment with our highest desires.

Knowledge is power. Knowing how your mind works allows you to direct it to deliver your desires. Understanding your resistance to change shifts your focus and gives you the key to overcoming it.

Introduction: The Power of Your Mind

Do you know how your mind works? If you did, you could harness and master its power. You'd be able to accomplish anything and everything you desire. Your current situation is not permanent, and the power to change everything lies within the way you manage your mind.

This is a fact.

The information in this book will explain how your mind works. After reading and absorbing this, you will understand—and then be able to harness—your own mind's power. You will be able to direct it toward your desired results.

Of course, there are a few other things to learn, but this is the groundwork to get there. Enjoy!

If we had been taught about the different parts of our mind at a young age and how to direct them, we would have been able to manifest whatever we desired. We would have the tools to direct our minds, fire up our intuition, and take the right actions to get there. Since we weren't taught this, we either struggle for years until we figure it out or live this life at the whims of events.

Knowledge is power. By understanding how your mind works, you can direct it to deliver your desires. Understanding your resistance to change gives you a different focus.

Our mind is very powerful and has many parts with different responsibilities. By learning how they work and their jobs, we can also learn how to manipulate our own brains.

THE MIND:

It is essential to understand how each part works so that we can understand and utilize their strengths.

- The Ego

- The Conscious Mind

- The Unconscious Mind

- The Subconscious Mind

- The SuperConscious Mind

THE EGO:

The ego will always tell you that you cannot have this or that, can't do this or that, because of whatever programming you received as a child. This could be that you aren't capable, aren't worthy, don't deserve it, ETC.

Your ego will also stop you because it is afraid you will delete it. Once you understand the ego's job, it will not be able to stop you from living your best life. Unless, of course, you let it. Understanding your resistance to change gives clarity, and there is a way to make this useful. The resistance is the very tension that we need in order to create.

The ego is a central player in how the mind operates, especially in relation to identity, perception, and resistance to change. Here are some key insights into how the ego functions:

1. **The Ego as the "Identity Keeper"**

    *   The ego forms a personal identity based on experiences, beliefs, and conditioning.
    *   It creates the sense of "I" and separates the self from others to maintain a unique identity.
    *   This self-image is rigid and doesn't like being questioned or changed.

2. **The Ego and Survival Mechanism**

    *   The ego's primary job is protection, ensuring survival by filtering reality through past experiences.
    *   It categorizes experiences as safe or threatening, even when the threat is only emotional, not physical.
    *   It operates based on fear of loss, failure, and rejection, keeping people in their comfort zones.

3. **The Ego Resists Change**

    *   The ego fears being "deleted" or dissolved, as it equates change with loss of identity.
    *   It clings to old beliefs, habits, and conditioning, even when they are harmful.
    *   It uses excuses, self-sabotage, and distractions to prevent personal growth.

4. **The Ego and Control**

    *   The ego thrives on control and predictability—it dislikes uncertainty.

- It creates false narratives to maintain a sense of certainty (e.g., "I can't do this," "I am not good enough").

- It seeks external validation to reinforce its beliefs and self-worth.

5. **The Ego and Perception Distortion**

   - The ego filters reality through biases, deleting, distorting, and generalizing information.

   - It takes things personally, even when they are not personal.

   - It projects assumptions onto people and situations based on past experiences.

6. **The Ego and Comparison**

   - The ego constantly compares itself to others to determine self-worth.

   - It creates feelings of superiority or inferiority, depending on the situation.

   - Social media, competition, and cultural standards feed the ego's need for validation.

7. **The Ego as the Creator of Duality**

   - The ego perceives the world in black and white, good and bad, success and failure.

   - It creates separation between self and others, leading to judgment, conflict, and division.

   - It feeds fear-based thinking—you must "win" or "lose," be "right" or "wrong."

8. **The Ego and Time (Past & Future Focus)**

   - The ego does not exist in the present moment; it is always reliving the past or worrying about the future.

- It replays past traumas, regrets, and mistakes, keeping people stuck.

- It creates anxiety about the future, fearing loss or failure before it even happens.

9. **The Ego and Emotional Triggers**

- The ego holds onto emotional wounds and reacts defensively when those wounds are touched.

- It creates anger, guilt, shame, or resentment when reality doesn't match expectations.

- It uses blame and justification to avoid personal responsibility.

10. **The Ego Can Be Rewired and Aligned**

- The ego is not the enemy but simply a program running outdated patterns.

- It can be rewired through awareness, inner work, and shifting perspectives.

- By disidentifying from the ego, we step into higher consciousness (superconscious awareness) and create new possibilities.

Final Thought:

The ego is a tool, but it should not be the master. Awareness is key—by observing the ego's patterns, we can dismantle limiting beliefs, shift our identity, and align with our true nature. This is key to manifesting our desires!

THE CONSCIOUS MIND:

1. **The Conscious Mind (Beta Frequency)**

   - The conscious mind is the part of your awareness that thinks, reasons, and makes decisions.

   - It holds one thought at a time and processes external reality through logic and sensory input.

   - It is the "gatekeeper" that decides what information gets passed to the subconscious.

   - The conscious mind can be neutral, logical, or even detached from emotions at times.

2. **The Ego (Identity & Self-Image)**

   - The ego is a construct of the mind, specifically a collection of beliefs, identities, and self-perceptions.

   - It operates as the "self" you believe you are—your identity, roles, and personality.

   - The ego filters reality based on past conditioning and seeks control, validation, and survival.

   - Unlike the neutral nature of the conscious mind, the ego is highly emotional and defensive when its identity is challenged.

Key Differences Between the Conscious Mind and the Ego:

Feature	Conscious Mind	Ego
Function	Thinks, reasons, makes decisions	Protects identity, defends beliefs
Awareness	Present-focused, logical	Past- and future-focused, emotional
Flexibility	Can change beliefs through logic and awareness	Resists change to protect self-identity
Reaction to Challenges	Can analyze and adapt	Gets defensive, avoids being "wrong"
Perception of Reality	Open to possibilities	Distorts, generalizes and personalizes

How They Interact:

- The ego uses the conscious mind to justify its beliefs and maintain control.

- The conscious mind can override the ego when a person is self-aware. This is key to success.

- The ego thrives in fear and separation, while the conscious mind can access higher awareness and rational thought.

Final Thought:

The ego is a function of the mind; however, it is not the entirety of the conscious mind. Think of the conscious mind as the driver and the ego as the backseat driver—if unchecked, the ego can hijack your thoughts, but with awareness, you can regain control.

When we are presented with a question or statement, the conscious mind decides what to do with it. It stops new ideas from coming in that do not align with our beliefs that were formed in childhood. Whatever you saw, heard, felt, tasted, and was recorded in your mind from the moment you were conceived. You recorded everything. There was no reference because we are born with amnesia. So, there was no way to understand anything logically. We just buy it. All of it. And being that your conscious mind sees everything in a pessimistic light, that explains why it is a challenge to decide otherwise.

When we are told "don't," the conscious mind does not hear this word. For example, don't touch the paint; don't touch the stove, it's hot. And what do we typically do? Some say that the ego is such a child; it just will not listen and will plow forward regardless of the danger. The ego just wants its way and will have it if left unchecked. Either way, the results are the same if it hears "don't" or chooses to ignore.

The conscious mind deletes, distorts, and generalizes everything. Once something gets past it, the conscious mind must make sense of it. This is where we get one side of the story. For example, there are four corners with a person on each corner. Stop signs for each corner. A car comes through as another car does as well and they hit. How many different versions of this occurrence are there? Which one is the truth?

THE SUBCONSCIOUS MIND (THE AUTOPILOT)

- The subconscious is the storage center for all learned behaviors, habits, emotions, and beliefs.

- It operates below conscious awareness but can be accessed with techniques like hypnosis, meditation, or deep focus.

- It processes all sensory input, past experiences, and automatic behaviors.

- Examples of subconscious functions:
  - Driving without thinking about every movement.
  - Instantly feeling fear or joy based on past experiences.
  - Muscle memory (playing an instrument, typing, etc.).

The subconscious learns through repetition and conditioning— once a behavior is learned, it runs on autopilot.

THE UNCONSCIOUS MIND (THE HIDDEN DEPTHS)

- The unconscious mind is even deeper than the subconscious.
- It contains buried memories, traumas, and instinctual drives that are not easily accessible.
- It is responsible for survival instincts, automatic body functions, and repressed experiences.
- Examples of unconscious functions:
  - Suppressed childhood trauma that affects adult relationships.

- Breathing, digestion, and heart rate (autonomic functions).

- Deep-seated fears or biases are formed before conscious awareness.

The unconscious mind protects you by hiding specific experiences or emotions until you're ready to process them. If a trauma or deeply emotional experience is too overwhelming, the unconscious mind suppresses it, preventing it from interfering with daily life. However, these suppressed experiences can still influence behavior, fears, and emotional responses without conscious awareness.

KEY DIFFERENCES BETWEEN THE SUBCONSCIOUS AND UNCONSCIOUS MIND

Feature	Subconscious Mind	Unconscious Mind
Awareness Level	Below conscious awareness but accessible	Deeply hidden, not easily accessed
Function	Stores habits, beliefs, and emotions	Holds instincts, traumas, and autonomic functions
How It Learns	Repetition, conditioning, sensory experiences	Protects and suppresses overwhelming experiences
Access Methods	Meditation, hypnosis, NLP, repetition	Deep therapy, trauma work, and spontaneous recall
Example Behaviors	Automatic driving, learned fears, muscle memory	Suppressed childhood trauma, survival instincts

How They Work Together

1. The subconscious is like a hard drive—it stores information, habits, and learned behaviors you use daily.

2. The unconscious is like an underground vault—it holds deeper emotions, instincts, and repressed memories that may influence behavior without your awareness.

3. Sometimes, unconscious content leaks into the subconscious (e.g., emotional triggers, irrational fears, dreams).

4. Healing and rewiring the mind often involve making the unconscious conscious—bringing awareness to hidden patterns so they can be changed.

Final Thought

The subconscious mind is programmable, while the unconscious mind is protective. By understanding both, we can direct our minds to our heart's desires, make traumas have no affect and also choose how we react to everything in life.

Aspect	Ego	Conscious Mind	Unconscious Mind
Awareness Level	Partially conscious	Fully conscious	Deeply hidden, not easily accessed
Function	Maintains identity, seeks validation, defends beliefs	Thinks, reasons, and makes logical decisions	Stores suppressed memories, instincts, autonomic functions
How It Learns	Reinforced by experiences, social conditioning	Learns through logic, observation, sensory input	Protects by hiding overwhelming experiences

---

This is all important and interesting, as it shows that when we know how to make demands, the superconscious and the unconscious will all follow those demands.

THE SUPERCONSCIOUS MIND

- The superconscious is a field of information above time and space. It:

- Is pure memory and intelligence
- Instructs the unconscious on what to do
- Has no thoughts or emotions
- Exists beyond logic and reason
- When we understand how to direct the superconscious, the unconscious will follow.

So, Who's in Charge?

Your conscious awareness is the Master Gardener of your mind, operating in Beta frequency.

The soil is your unconscious mind, which takes orders from both the conscious and the superconscious.

Manifestation begins in the superconscious. It changes the connections in your brain's neurons. The language patterns in your mind create coding sequences—when these sequences are run consistently, they become automatic processes.

You must scramble the old coding if you want to change your subconscious patterns. Imagine a scratched CD—it can't play the same song anymore. Similarly, rewiring your brain disrupts limiting patterns and allows new perspectives to form.

How Our Perception is Formed

As children, we learn that we are individuals, separate from the whole.

The unconscious mind takes everything personally, shaping its beliefs from ages 0 to 4. This is when we absorb limiting beliefs about who we are and what is possible.

Most adults never break free from these unconscious limitations. Society lives in an amnesic state, operating from childhood programming.

However, we can consciously shift out of this once we recognize it.

How Our Brain Processes Reality

Whenever we see, hear, feel, taste, or experience something, our brain searches for reference points:

Is it safe or dangerous?

- Have we experienced this before?

- What do we think, feel, and believe about it?

If there's no reference point, our brain creates one. At that moment, we can either:

Follow our old conditioning (domestication)

Or

Consciously create a new belief or perspective

However, our brains naturally delete, distort, and generalize information.

For example, your brain doesn't hear the word "don't." If someone says, "Don't touch the stove; it's hot," your brain focuses on "Touch the stove." This is why we often end up doing exactly what we were told not to. There is another theory out there that the ego doesn't like to be told no, so it just loses control and does it anyway.

Similarly, when you say, "I don't want to be broke," your brain hears, "I want to be broke."

Your words matter—they shape your subconscious programming.

Most memories remain dormant, but they can be reactivated when triggered.

For example, if I ask, "When was the last time you stubbed your toe?" your brain retrieves the memory instantly. This proves that our past shapes our present responses.

Healing & Rewiring the Mind

There is a dissociation process between the conscious and unconscious mind.

Many of our daily actions, like driving, happen automatically.

- Trauma can also create separate parts of our mind, storing emotional triggers that may resurface later.

The superconscious can heal trauma parts by removing negative emotions and replacing them with neutral or positive emotions. This process is usually painless and leads to greater satisfaction in life.

Final Thoughts: Step Into Your Power

To create by magic, you must constantly challenge your perception, uncover your truth, and take action.

We live in a world of illusions and distorted reality.

Like a fish in the ocean, we must rise above the surface and orient ourselves toward the truth.

So, who's in charge?

You are.

Now, let's begin.

Let's Put This Into Action:

Write down something you would like to accomplish. What is the first thought that comes into your mind? Perhaps your ego is telling you that you aren't capable. You aren't worthy? Don't belong? Not perfect enough? Not good enough? Not significant? Right now, write down what you are telling yourself about how you can't do or have this, and why? Be as honest as you can, without judgment. Be as compassionate with yourself as you can. This is to identify and become aware of how quickly the message of why you are not able to do something comes through.

We operate from a few of these spaces, and we will be figuring out which ones are the primary modes of operation so that when we hear ourselves saying or telling ourselves one of them, we will know that it is the ego speaking. Not our powerful selves!

This is where you either listen to it or ignore it. If you have listened to it, it will not matter how many affirmations you say, mantras, breathing, or meditation. Because your subconscious believes that first thought and will not allow you to achieve whatever it is you would like to accomplish. No matter what actions you take or how far forward you get, your subconscious will always take you back to that first thought. It is hard-wired in your brain. Your brain looks for reasons to prove you can't have what you desire. It will prove it over and over again. Until you learn how to get around this, this is what happens.

Whatever you focus on is your reality. The ego is relentless and brings you back to the thought that you aren't capable, etc. It proves it again and again. Until you harness the ability to choose differently and focus on your desires, this is possible, and you will have a handle on this after you read this book. The tools you will learn will allow you to be aware of the ego's message, and you will be able to shift into your amazing creative self!

"The mind is like a parachute. It doesn't work if it is not open." — Frank Zappa

You can't see it, but it controls everything. You can train it, but it resists.

Which part of your mind is running the show right now—your subconscious, your ego, or your conscious self?

Mind Components Comparison

Aspect	Ego	Conscious Mind	Unconscious Mind	Subconscious Mind
Awareness Level	Partially conscious	Fully conscious	Deeply hidden, not easily accessed	Below conscious awareness but accessible
Function	Maintains identity, seeks validation, defends beliefs	Thinks, reasons, makes logical decisions	Stores suppressed memories, instincts, autonomic functions	Stores habits, beliefs, emotions, and automatic behaviors
How It Learns	Reinforced by experiences, social conditioning	Learns through logic, observation, sensory input	Protects by hiding overwhelming experiences	Learns through repetition, conditioning, sensory experiences
Access Methods	Self-reflection, mindfulness, shadow work	Awareness, focus, problem-solving	Deep therapy, trauma work, spontaneous recall	Meditation, hypnosis, NLP, repetition
Example Behaviors	Defensive reactions, comparison, self-judgment	Analyzing situations, making decisions, problem-solving	Repressed trauma, instinctual fears, body functions	Driving on autopilot, learned fears, muscle memory
Primary Focus	Self-image, survival in social structures	Present-moment awareness, logical thought	Survival, protection from distress	Automation of thoughts, behaviors, and emotions
Emotional Influence	Highly emotional, takes things personally	Can be neutral, but influenced by emotions	Strong emotional charge but operates in the background	Influences emotions but does not reason

Decision-Making Ability	Rationalizes choices to align with self-image	Makes deliberate choices based on reason	Influences decisions un-consciously	Runs automatic behaviors, minimal conscious control

Go to the **ENNEAGRAM QUIZ** in the workbook. Use the quiz in the workbook to identify your egoic agendas. Once you have taken the quiz, write your enneagram type in your journal.

Enneagram Types & Their Manifestation Blocks

This is a summary of enneagram types, their blocks, the expansive aspects, and the manifestation key. It is highly recommended to learn even more about enneagrams for a thorough understanding of what egoic agenda is running. Now you have identified your egoic agenda. Make a note of yours in your journal, as you will use this information for insight.

Type 1 – The Perfectionist / Reformer

- **Negative Aspects:** Perfectionistic, judgmental, critical of self and others, overly rigid or self-righteous. Believes everything must be perfect before taking action.

- **Positive Aspects:** Principled, responsible, self-disciplined, motivated by a strong sense of justice and integrity.

- **Shifting for Manifestation:** Release the need to be perfect. Focus on inspired action instead of control. Accept progress over perfection.

Manifestation Key: Let "good enough" be powerful. Manifestation flows when you trust your worth in the now, not in a flawless future.

Type 2 – The Helper / Giver

- **Negative Aspects:** People-pleasing, self-sacrificing, manipulative when unacknowledged, neglects personal desires—struggles to receive.

- **Positive Aspects:** Warm, caring, generous, and attuned to others' needs.

- **Shifting for Manifestation:** Prioritize self-worth. Recognize that your needs matter and that abundance doesn't require earning through service.

Manifestation Key: You are worthy of receiving simply because you exist. Allow in love, wealth, and joy without guilt or overgiving.

Type 3 – The Achiever / Performer

- **Negative Aspects:** Over-identifies with success, seeks validation, overly image-conscious. Turns manifestation into performance.

- **Positive Aspects:** Driven, efficient, adaptable, and results-oriented.

- **Shifting for Manifestation:** Detach from external measures. Define success from your soul's truth, not others' approval.

Manifestation Key: Manifest through alignment, not achievement. Let your desires come from authenticity—not performance.

Type 4 – The Individualist / Romantic

- **Negative Aspects:** Melancholic, envious, emotionally intense, believes suffering creates depth or meaning. Feels misunderstood.

- **Positive Aspects:** Creative, expressive, introspective, emotionally rich, and deeply intuitive.

- **Shifting for Manifestation:** Release attachment to emotional struggle. Create from joy and beauty instead of pain.

Manifestation Key: Step into the joy of being seen and fulfilled. Let manifestation be easeful, not dramatic.

Type 5 – The Investigator / Observer

- **Negative Aspects:** Withdrawn, secretive, overly analytical, emotionally detached. Gets stuck in thought, avoids taking action.

- **Positive Aspects:** Insightful, observant, independent, able to understand deep systems and patterns.

- **Shifting for Manifestation:** Trust that you don't need all the data before moving. Feel safe taking small, imperfect steps.

Manifestation Key: Manifestation happens through experience, not analysis. Use intuition as much as intellect—act on inner knowing.

Type 6 – The Loyalist / Guardian

- **Negative Aspects:** Fear-driven, overly anxious, skeptical, seeks external security, distrustful of self. May over-prepare, doubt intuition, and seek certainty before moving forward.

- **Positive Aspects:** Loyal, dependable, committed, prepared, protective, and supportive. Deep inner strength and capacity to anticipate and respond to challenges.

- **Shifting for Manifestation:** Trust in your inner guidance and in life itself. Security comes from alignment, not external guarantees.

Manifestation Key: Feel the fear and move anyway. Ground yourself in faith. Build inner safety so you can take bold steps and magnetize with confidence.

Type 7 – The Enthusiast / Visionary

- **Negative Aspects:** Avoids pain by staying busy or chasing the next thrill. Scattered, impatient, avoids commitment, overindulgent, and distracted by too many options.

- **Positive Aspects:** Joyful, optimistic, spontaneous, innovative, and full of ideas. Brings energy and enthusiasm to any vision.

- **Shifting for Manifestation:** Slow down and get clear on one aligned desire. Depth creates power.

Manifestation Key: Focus your energy. Choose one desire and follow through with presence. Joy and excitement are tools—use them to anchor, not escape.

Type 8 – The Challenger / Protector

- **Negative Aspects:** Controlling, aggressive, confrontational, unwilling to show vulnerability. May resist surrender and try to force manifestations through intensity.
- **Positive Aspects:** Strong, protective, assertive, courageous, and willing to fight for justice and truth. Embodies powerful leadership.
- **Shifting for Manifestation:** Let go of the need to control. Power flows best when paired with openness.

Manifestation Key: Use your strength to protect—not push. Soften into trust. Manifest by commanding with clarity, then allowing with grace.

Type 9 – The Peacemaker / Mediator

- **Negative Aspects:** Avoids conflict, disconnects from personal desires, numbs out or procrastinates. Overly accommodating and may merge with others' goals.
- **Positive Aspects:** Calm, accepting, grounded, diplomatic, and able to see all sides. Creates harmony and stability.
- **Shifting for Manifestation:** Your desires matter. Wake up to them and take action.

Manifestation Key: Get clear on what you want. Speak it, claim it, and move toward it consistently. Your presence is powerful when fully engaged.

CHAPTER 2

GOOD CHOICES VS. ALIGNED CHOICES

Your next level of success starts with an aligned choice—are you ready?

Choices are the foundation of your success. Every day, we make countless choices—some small and seemingly insignificant, others life-changing. What to wear, where to go, what to do, what to eat, what to drink, when to sleep, who we surround ourselves with, and more. What if the power of the type of choice is the key to unlocking everything you desire? All these choices make up what our life experiences are. When we are in alignment, these choices that we make bring us joy, bring us happiness, and bring us our desires.

The Truth About Choices

Most people think they are making conscious decisions, but in reality, many choices are influenced by subconscious patterns, fears, and limiting beliefs. If you've ever felt stuck, frustrated, or unable to break through to the next level, it's not because you lack discipline or motivation—it's because your choices are being guided by old programming. Something you've probably heard many times. We make choices consciously, unconsciously, and subconsciously without having all the information as to why we would choose something.

Good Choices vs. Aligned Choices

A "good" choice isn't necessarily the right one for you. Instead of making choices based on what seems logical, practical, or expected, or from the space of what you are lacking, The Success Zones teaches and guides you to make aligned choices—decisions that resonate with your true self and lead to effortless success.

So, how do you genuinely shift your choices to Aligned Choices vs. simply Good Ones?

How Choice Shapes Your Reality

- Your Thoughts → Your Choices → Your Actions → Your Reality

  The results you see in your life today reflect the choices you've made in the past. When you shift your choices, you absolutely will shift your reality.

- The Power of Awareness

  The first step to transformation is recognizing where your choices are coming from. Are they based on fear or freedom? Are they moving you toward expansion or keeping you stuck?

Making a true choice, one you are in total alignment with, leads to success and fulfillment. The importance of making a choice aligned with our hearts and souls cannot be emphasized enough. When you realize where you are making choices from (either the ego, conscious mind, unconscious mind, subconscious, or superconscious mind) and then understand and know how to direct your mind, this is where the power is. Even choosing where you are making your choices from is a choice.

This is where the magic is.

We can choose to say no to ourselves or to say yes. Saying yes to things you only imagine is a leap of faith in yourself. It is a way of acknowledging that your superconscious will find a way for you to have your desires. It may not show up like you think it should or could; it usually shows up even better than you can imagine. Especially when you learn to listen, follow, and allow your superconscious to bring your desires to you.

We often say no because we think we can't afford it, we don't have time, we don't know how, we don't (blank). This shuts down any opportunity for your superconscious to even attempt bringing what you might have said yes to, except for all your stories. Saying no stops all flow. Saying yes to something even though you have no idea how, when, or where you can have whatever it is you are saying yes to allows your superconscious to bring about the desire. When you say yes and don't know how, your superconscious will bring the people and resources so that your desire comes to fruition. Yes, it is that simple. Have faith in yourself. *Say yes to you!*

Notice I said follow, which means listening to and taking action on what you hear when you ask what is next. Learning to trust your intuition is key here. Asking every day about what you can do to get your desires and listening to what you hear is critical to getting to your desired end game. It can even be counterintuitive. How many times in your life have you NOT listened to your intuition and kicked yourself in the butt because you knew??? How to listen to your intuition is covered in another chapter.

So, the question to ask yourself is, "What action can I take today to get where I want to go?"

Listen with an open heart and follow the action. If you don't follow the action and are aware, don't worry; there are endless opportunities provided in life.

Your Operating System:

Do you recognize where you operate from? At this point, you should have done the enneagram quiz and learned your egoic agenda and where you operate from. This is helpful to know, to recognize. It is okay that we operate from egoic agendas. The ego just wants to keep you safe. It is important to understand that when the egoic agenda shows up, you observe it, thank it for sharing its concerns, and move forward anyway. It is not a judgment; it is not a detriment. It just is the way you operate. When we observe it in action and decide to go forward and *not* listen to it, this is where we have chosen to be in our superconscious power, which is how we get to our desires. It is also helpful to understand where others are operating from. Understanding that also allows for accepting others' journeys, allowing others to be on their own journey.

For example, one of my desires was to write a book—this book. So I chose to write it. My ego told me that no one wants to read what I have to write, that I don't know enough, and that I'm not good enough. My conscious mind provided its own doubts, my unconscious mind had its fears, and my subconscious carried limiting beliefs. However, I chose to do it anyway. I focused on my desired reality. I didn't listen to my doubts. Every day, I asked, "What action can I take to get there?" I listened, I followed the intuition, and here we are—you are reading my book.

Ways We Create Ineffective Choices

When we choose from the heart, we do not have any limitations. We only choose what seems possible. This is also limiting, as our ego doesn't think we can do much of anything. When we choose the process instead of the result, this is also ineffective. We are not seeing or being in the desired outcome; we are just taking the steps we think are necessary to get where we want to go. This doesn't work because we are focused on the process, not the desire. When we choose something just to choose also doesn't work because our hearts are not in it. We are not in alignment. When we make choices based on reaction, thinking that this will resolve a conflict is another ineffective way to make a choice. If you want to be a problem solver, the universe and your superconscious will bring you problem after problem to solve. There is no need to solve a problem. Decide what the outcome you would like to be and have is, and that is the aligned choice. When you make a conditional choice, this is also ineffective. You say you will choose this or do this if this shows up. This is not an aligned choice. And if you just follow everyone or someone, that is also not an effective choice. That is giving up any choice at all. And you will never have what you desire.

Aligning With Your True Choice

What resistance is there? What inner conflicts? What judgments? What emotions prevent you? What are your stories? What benefits do you get from this resistance? Now, take ownership of the fact that you have created this experience. Be kind about it; no judging!

Again, choices should never be driven by what you do not have. When we recognize that our identity often prevents us from stepping into our power, it becomes necessary to acknowledge it without giving it control. Expose and acknowledge your resistance. Expand the vibration of your true end result and choose that. Making an aligned choice is critical to success.

Now, go to the workbook, do the exercises, and listen to the Field of Infinite Possibilities Meditation (or read it). You may also record the meditation in your own voice. Then, head back here and finish this chapter.

The Three States of Choice: Flip-Flopping, Blocked, and Free Flowing

Imagine being on a river in a canoe. Do you attempt to go upstream against the current? Or do you realize how difficult that would be and choose to flow with the river? This is the same when we make choices. When they align with our hearts, our minds will look for everything to make it happen. And yes, our egos can say what they want. Just thank your ego and keep focusing on your desires.

What you focus on becomes your reality. This is a choice as well. We decide what we focus on. However, you may find yourself:

- **Flip-flopping:** Almost getting there but always coming back to where you started. This happens because you are working from a negative vision, attempting to escape something rather than move toward something.

- **Blocked**: Not seeing results because of an opposing belief stopping you.

- **Free flowing:** Achieving success effortlessly because you have a pure vision and a true choice born from a clear end result.

The ego holds us back because it has a lifelong agenda. Where you operate from was determined when you took the quiz to see where your ego operates from. This keeps us stuck trying to "fix" ourselves rather than moving forward. Once we learn to accept that there will be some discomfort, see it for what it is, and still choose to focus on our desired reality, we unlock our true power. Once we really get that, we do not need to fix anything but our focus; that is when we step into our power. Our power of being an extraordinary creative force.

It is that simple. Focus on the desired outcome and ignore the ego. Trust that your superconscious has it handled. It does an amazing job when we allow our superconscious to go forth and find the answers and solutions for our desires to come to fruition. We will always be surprised when what we desire shows up even better than we could imagine. Just by allowing it to come forth. By listening to what actions to take and following your superconscious lead.

Which one of these describes your superconscious self?

Innovative Visionary – Someone who sees beyond the ordinary and creates groundbreaking ideas.

Masterful Creator – A person with an exceptional ability to bring unique ideas to life.

Brilliant Problem-Solver – Someone who finds unconventional and ingenious solutions.

Inspired Thinker – A mind that generates fresh, transformative perspectives.

Artistic Trailblazer – A person who pioneers new creative expressions.

Imaginative Luminary – A guiding force of originality and inspiration.

Visionary Architect – One who constructs new realities through boundless creativity.

Inventive Genius – A thinker who produces original and game-changing concepts.

Expressive Innovator – A creator who reshapes the world with their ideas.

A Boundless Dreamer – Someone whose creativity knows no limits.

In addition to focusing and listening, anchoring your desired reality is to feel it and see it—to fully embody it with every part of your being. This makes focusing easier; it becomes real when you feel it and see it. When you achieve the desired result, your superconsciousness makes it so.

- The Ego may resist, telling you why it's impossible or why you don't deserve it. It clings to past limitations and doubts, trying to keep you in the familiar.

- The Conscious Mind will analyze, question, and attempt to rationalize your vision, sometimes aligning with it but often seeking proof before belief.

- The Unconscious Mind stores deep-seated patterns and automatic responses, filtering what it believes is possible based on past experiences. It may initially hold hidden resistance but can be reprogrammed.

- The Subconscious Mind governs emotions, habits, and beliefs, responding most powerfully to the feelings and images you consistently engage with. When you feel and see your desired reality as real, the subconscious begins to accept it as truth.

- The Subconscious Mind operates beyond limitations, holding the infinite potential for creation. It connects you to intuitive insights, synchronicities, and inspired action, effortlessly guiding you toward your desired reality.

When all aspects of your mind are aligned—when you override the ego's doubts, train the subconscious with elevated emotions, and trust the superconscious to orchestrate the path—your vision moves from a mere thought to an undeniable reality.

In short, when you have your true goals, focusing on the desire for them is key. It is not necessary to change your beliefs or identity. Focus on the desires. Choose your desire or goal because you would just love to have it, love to be it, and love to do it.

The greatest creative force in the world lies in the emotion of the true end result. The more you focus on your true desired reality, the more the identity holding you back steps aside. This means you do not have to change, because you are not broken. One only has to focus on their true desires. How often have you "cleared" something, and it comes back? That is the point. Those personality traits are permanent; the beliefs are always there. We just get to decide if we believe them when they pop up, let them stop us from having our heart's desires, or say thanks for sharing and focus on our heart's desires. Making choices and taking inspired action gets you where you want to go. The importance of making a true choice cannot be emphasized enough. Attach no negative energy to your choice, and you will step into the life you truly desire. When making your aligned choice, it needs to be clear and precise. For example, if my choice was to write a successful book, a highly sold book, this immediately brings up subconsciously that fact that I don't think or believe that my book will be successful. So, the clear, aligned choice is that I desire to write a book. Period.

> *"Be careful what you water your dreams with."*
>
> — *Dodinsky*
>
> Imagine you wake up with no memory but a blank slate and $10 million in the bank.
>
> What would you "choose" to desire—if nobody else's opinions mattered?

CHAPTER 3

HEART-GUIDED WRITING

Now that you know how to make choices rooted in what you truly love and desire, free from doubts about possibility, the need for a plan, or reactions to what you don't want, you can create a vision guided purely by your heart's authentic calling.

The heart and brain maintain a dynamic, bidirectional relationship, communicating through intricate neural pathways and biochemical signals. This connection influences not only physiological functions but also emotional and cognitive processes.

Neural Communication Between Heart and Brain

The autonomic nervous system (ANS) regulates involuntary bodily functions. It comprises two main branches: The Sympathetic Nervous System (SNS) prepares the body for 'fight or flight' responses by increasing heart rate and blood pressure. The Parasympathetic Nervous System (PNS): promotes 'rest and digest' activities, primarily mediated by the vagus nerve, which decreases heart rate and facilitates relaxation.

The vagus nerve, or the tenth cranial nerve, is pivotal in heart-brain communication. It transmits parasympathetic signals to and from the heart, lungs, and digestive tract, influencing heart rate variability (HRV). HRV refers to the variation in time intervals between consecutive heartbeats and serves as an indicator of autonomic nervous system balance. Higher HRV is associated with greater adaptability and resilience to stress, reflecting a healthy balance between SNS and PNS activity.

Intrinsic Cardiac Nervous System

Beyond neural inputs from the brain, the heart possesses its own intrinsic cardiac nervous system, often termed the "heart's little brain." This complex network consists of approximately 40,000 neurons that can sense, process, and relay information independently of the central nervous system. It regulates heart rhythms and has the capacity to influence emotional and cognitive processes, underscoring the heart's role beyond mere circulation.

The heart and brain communicate continuously and complexly through neural, hormonal, and electromagnetic pathways. Understanding this interplay is crucial for comprehending how emotional, cognitive, and physiological processes are integrated and influence overall health and well-being.

Now, let's connect with our hearts so that we can deeply feel what having our desires feels like. Our hearts have desires, and this is how we can learn to listen. Are you ready to listen to your heart's desires?

Turn to the workbook and read, listen to, or record the Journey to Knowing Meditation.

> *"When you are in alignment with who you truly are, things just flow."*
>
> — *Abraham-Hicks*
>
> A river doesn't try to flow—it just does. What if "trying harder" is actually blocking your flow?

CHAPTER 4
YOUR SHADOW

The shadow side refers to the unconscious aspects of ourselves that we repress, deny, or disown. This concept originates from Carl Jung's work, where he described the shadow as the part of our psyche that contains all the traits, emotions, and desires we reject because they are deemed unacceptable by society, family, or our own self-image.

The shadow consists of hidden or suppressed parts of our personality. It includes our fears, insecurities, anger, envy, selfishness, and even unexpressed creativity and power. It forms during childhood when we begin filtering what is "good" and "bad" based on external expectations. The more we reject aspects of ourselves, the more they show up in subconscious ways—like self-sabotage, projection, or inner turmoil.

The shadow manifests in daily life in various forms. When we judge or criticize others for qualities we secretly possess but refuse to acknowledge (e.g., calling someone arrogant when we suppress our own confidence), this is projection.

When we are triggered emotionally, it may point to a shadow aspect we have not integrated.

Our shadow side may unconsciously hold us back from success or happiness if we believe we are unworthy. This is self-sabotage.

Unhealed shadows lead to recurring relationship struggles, as we either attract people who reflect our shadow or push others away to avoid facing it. Our brains are wired to look for relationships and conflicts in order to prove that the ego is correct.

Feelings of guilt or shame often arise when we suppress parts of ourselves, we secretly desire but were taught to reject.

Ignoring the shadow leads to inner conflict, low self-esteem, and self-sabotage. However, when we integrate our shadow, we are able to live an empowered life. We experience greater self-acceptance and inner peace. We break cycles of negative behaviors and self-sabotage. We develop deeper self-awareness and authenticity. We strengthen relationships by taking responsibility for our projections. We unlock hidden strengths, creativity, and confidence.

By noticing your triggers, just observing yourself with no judgment, write down the things that irritate you most in other people. Write down what emotions are uncomfortable for you to feel. What are the recurring patterns in your life? In relationships, what is your career, and what is your personal life? Just be an observer. Ponder on where you judge others harshly. All of this information reveals the aspects of yourself that you deny.

Take some time daily to write down your fears for the day, desires you denied yourself, and emotions you shoved down. Just observe. Just follow the trail of where these observations take you. When did you first feel this way? What parts of you are you ashamed of? When were you rejected? When were you angry? When were you envious? Just reflect. Don't judge!

I talk to myself all the time. Some of the best conversations I've had are with myself. If you haven't already, let's start. Ask your shadow questions. What would your shadow say to you if you listened? Read the meditation below and then write a letter from your shadow to you and a letter to your shadow from yourself.

Please note that the shadow is not bad; it is a part of you that can hold space for things you need to understand and heal. That is its job. However, just like the ego, sometimes it stops us from having our desires. Reconciliation of all parts is key to choosing and executing your will.

What we decide and believe was created long before we were online. For example, it is not okay for a male to cry, and everyone in society has made sure this is so. What if those tears were powerful and necessary? What we think of as being a weakness can be our strength, a barometer into our soul. Loving oneself means loving each and every single part of you! After all, it is all the parts that make a whole!

Creativity expands, confidence grows, and clarity and authenticity emerge when we allow ourselves to live a life we love.

Your shadow isn't the enemy—it's a portal to wholeness. By embracing and integrating it, you unlock your fullest potential and step into a life of greater alignment and authenticity.

When we love ourselves, we will no longer fear our dark side. By bringing it into the light, the fear is removed.

Until it tells you its truth, it has to stay in between worlds. When it can finally tell you about your power, when you truly get your dark side, it's allowed to go back to wherever it came from. This is its Dharma, its purpose. It has to sit in this suspension until it can tell you this. It's very important; it's very excited to share the dark side you've been hiding your whole life. When you meet it, you will be writing and deciphering, realizing this is what you have been asking for all along. The symbol you get will talk to you. Write what comes; don't judge it. If you aren't getting anything, just start writing.

Go to the workbook, read, listen, or record the Shadow Side Meditation, and do the journal work.

Give yourself a big hug, and embrace all of you! Freedom and peace are now yours!

> *"You don't get what you want. You get what you *are*."*
> — *Wayne Dyer*
>
> Two people have the same goal. One believes it's impossible. One believes it's inevitable. Who manifests it— and why?

CHAPTER 5

ALIGN ALL ENERGIES WITHIN

The Conscious Mind • The Unconscious Mind • The Subconscious Mind

It is a process of getting them to work together. We choose to instruct and choreograph the mind's different parts to achieve our dreams.

Now that we have uncovered your true goals and desires, tapped into your heart, and met your shadow, this chapter will show you some tools to bring your subconscious into complete harmony. This alignment ensures honesty and integrity with your deepest truths, removing any internal resistance. Without this alignment, the subconscious will block the manifestation of what you truly desire.

Life is flowing smoothly; you're making progress and feeling aligned, and then an unexpected challenge or setback disrupts your momentum, pulling you back into old patterns. Where you no longer wanted to be. What happened? Do you then keep focusing on your reality, or do you fall into the pit of despair and give up? This only shows you that you are not aligned with your desires and that your focus has shifted. When our focus shifts and lands on what you don't want, there are ways to shift your focus. Shifting your focus is key. And life will always attempt to shift your focus.

We often struggle to align with our desires and dreams because different parts of our mind operate with conflicting messages. The ego is always telling us "No", you can't. The conscious mind is responsible for logic and decision-making, the unconscious mind stores deep-seated patterns and automatic functions, and the subconscious mind acts as the bridge between the two, influencing behavior based on past conditioning and beliefs. The way we get them to work together is a process. We choose to instruct and choreograph the mind's different parts to achieve and reach our dreams.

When you are out of alignment, there are many clues in your life that point to this. Everything is wobbly like a car with out-of-balance tires; you can't get to where you want to go. You go left, right, forward, backward, or sideways, and it feels like you are on a roller coaster.

Ensuring you are aligned means tuning into your superconscious, the higher aspect of your awareness that connects you to intuition, wisdom, and a broader understanding of your path. Being able to listen to yourself is critical. Your higher self, your superconscious, allows you to follow inspired action. The Universe will bring you the people, the information, and all the things necessary for you to realize your desires. Yes, we must take inspired action and keep our focus on our desired goals. We do not need to know how to do it. At all! When we are aligned and focused, the Universe brings everything to us.

Instead of trying to paddle upstream, you are in flow. And no, not everything goes smoothly; life isn't like that. However, you will see that you are making progress despite the bumps in the road. When we choose to focus on our desired reality and our desires and keep focusing, this is the power of choice. This is key to getting where we desire to be, having what we desire, and being what we desire.

Your focus shapes your reality. Concentrating on something—whether positive or negative—expands your awareness. For example, if you fixate on a minor inconvenience, it can quickly feel overwhelming, whereas shifting your focus to a desired outcome can bring clarity and momentum. I want you to focus on your stomach. How big is it? How small is it? And as you keep focusing, what happens to your stomach? Does it become larger in your mind? What happens? Typically, it becomes so large we can't stand it, and then we spiral. Use any part of your body, use any experience, and just play with what happens when you focus on that alone.

Go to the workbook and do the Self-Reflection exercise. This exercise is useful for choosing and aligning all of your mind so that when you direct your subconscious and superconscious, they will have the leading role and provide access to your desires. The leading role of the superconscious and subconscious is key to success and direction; seeing where you are is powerful.

Final Thought:

Acknowledge the resilience, wisdom, and brilliance that have always been within you. Your awareness and perspective have the power to shift your experience.

Where's the power?

This exercise helps you see where the power is and choose which path to take. You can look at current issues objectively and then use your intuition to move through them. This is in total alignment with how your mind work with your heart.

Do this exercise whenever you need to change your focus, whenever you need to re-group, whenever you need help remembering where your power lies!

It is a wonderful place to learn how to refocus and take inspired action on our aligned desires and goals. It is empowering and comforting.

> *"Your intuition knows what to write, so get out of the way."*
>
> — *Ray Bradbury*
>
> You're lost in the woods. One path looks safe. One path feels right.
>
> Which do you take—and why?

CHAPTER 6

MANIFESTATION

Manifestation is done by directing your mind to follow your directions. This is where the magic is when we align choices and use the power of the different parts of the mind. This is where we change lead into gold: alchemy. Instead of battling the various parts of the mind, we know how to direct all energies into delivering our desires.

The Mind, Ego, and Manifestation

Knowing how the mind works is the foundation of manifestation. Understanding how you operate (through systems like the Enneagram) also plays a role. Acknowledging and accepting your natural tendencies allows you to direct your mind toward your desired goals. It is not always easy to accept what we consider the negative parts of ourselves. To embrace our shadow side. The shadow side and negative parts all have messages and are there to assist us. Once we understand that and embrace all of us, it gets easier to manifest. We will still be learning and building on the skills and information we have already covered, and this will make your manifestation of your desires happen.

When you set a new desire, your operating mode—your ego's agenda—appears immediately. Instead of resisting it, simply acknowledge its presence. Thank it for sharing, expressing gratitude for the information, and then shift your focus back to your desired outcome.

The ego's job is to protect your identity and reinforce your current beliefs, even if they no longer serve you. When you set a new desire, your ego may resist by offering limiting thoughts. Instead of fighting it, simply acknowledge it and redirect your focus.

The conscious mind helps you with reason and shifting perspectives. The subconscious mind is programmable, meaning it can be trained to support your goals. The unconscious mind operates from deep, protective instincts. By understanding these distinctions, you can retrain your subconscious and direct your focus to create the results you desire.

Affirmations sound wonderful. However, your mind hears you saying something that it knows isn't true and will go about making sure it proves this to you. You can repeat something as much as you like, but without focus and direction, your mind will not allow it.

Your enneagram does affect how you operate, and it does affect your manifestation process. If you let the ego run the program, however, you now understand that you can choose who runs the program.

15-Minute Daily Manifestation Practice

Start your day by selecting two of your key desires. Write them out. Close your eyes, take a deep breath, and ask yourself: **"What action can I take today to move closer to these desires?"**

Listen to the answer that comes up. Trust the first nudge you receive and take action on it, no matter how small. And no matter if it makes sense to you.

- Read through all of your desires and focus on the feelings they bring.
- Write down how each desire makes you feel—joyful, excited, at peace, etc.

- Visualize what you will be doing when you have achieved these things. Write these down as well.

- Write down what actions you are taking in your vision.

By focusing on your desires, asking for direction, listening, and taking inspired action, you allow manifestation to unfold with ease. There is no need to control the "how's."

Faith and trust are the foundation of this process. When you align and flow with your desires, heart, and purpose, you will begin to experience daily miracles. All the parts of your mind will also be directed to do their part.

The directions are in the workbook, along with a Daily Vision format. You can make your own or use this one.

Final Thought:

Acknowledge and accept your type's natural patterns. Understanding how you operate, how to shift out of ego-driven limitations, and how to manifest in a way that aligns with your personality is powerful. Use the 15-minute daily practice to integrate these insights and stay in alignment with your manifestation strengths. This allows you to move forward confidently and easily, creating the reality you desire.

"The only thing worse than being blind is having sight but no vision."

— Helen Keller

If you could only imagine one outcome today—positive or negative— which one would you choose to invest your energy in?

CHAPTER 7

INTUITION

Every second, our minds process 400 billion bits of information, yet we are consciously aware of only 2,000. How do we choose what to focus on? Instead of believing we are not creators, you'll discover the truth: you are. Harness this intuitive awareness to guide your daily actions, aligning them with your goals and desires.

How many times have you wished you had listened to your intuition? How often would you have avoided a conflict, a nasty situation, or a devastating experience?

Understanding Intuition: More Than Just a Feeling

Intuition isn't just a gut feeling—it's a form of intelligence that integrates subconscious processing, energetic awareness, and higher guidance. It's the synthesis of your life experiences, knowledge, and an unseen wisdom beyond logical reasoning.

Modern neuroscience shows that the brain gathers and processes far more information than our conscious mind can handle. Intuition is the result of this silent processing—signals from your nervous system, energetic alignment, and even collective consciousness guide you toward what serves you best.

The Science and Energy of Intuition

Intuition isn't magic—it's a highly sophisticated system involving your nervous system, heart intelligence, and subtle energetic perception. Scientists have found that the heart sends more signals to the brain than the brain does to the heart, influencing emotional and cognitive processes. This "heart-brain connection" plays a huge role in intuitive decision-making.

From an energetic perspective, intuition aligns with what spiritual traditions have called "higher knowing." It taps into the quantum field—a vast network of energy and intelligence beyond time and space—where answers and insights already exist. Your ability to access this field determines how much intuitive clarity you experience.

The Role of Intuition in The Success Zones

When you develop trust in your intuition, you unlock:

- **Clarity**: Decision-making becomes effortless and aligned.

- **Synchronicity**: The right people and opportunities show up.

- **Authenticity**: You move away from people-pleasing and conditioned responses.

- **Inner Peace**: You reduce overthinking and hesitation, knowing you are guided.

Many people struggle with intuition because they doubt themselves or override their inner knowing with logic or fear. The Success Zones teaches you how to break free from these limitations and fully trust your intuitive wisdom.

How to Strengthen Your Intuition

1. **Stillness & Presence:** Intuition speaks in silence, not in noise. Meditation, breathwork, or quiet walks enhance one's ability to hear it.

2. **Ask and Receive:** Develop a practice of asking your intuition simple questions and noticing how answers come to you (through sensations, dreams, or sudden insights).

3. **Trust Small Nudges:** Every time you act on a small, intuitive hit and see the results, your confidence in your intuition grows.

4. **Energetic Alignment:** Clear subconscious fears and resistance that block intuitive clarity.

5. **Body Awareness:** The body is a powerful, intuitive instrument. Learn to feel your body's "yes" and "no" signals.

The Genius Mode of Awareness

When you enter the Genius Mode of Awareness, you step beyond thoughts and emotions into pure knowing. This is a state of awe, where wisdom flows naturally, and fear no longer clouds your choices. By practicing intuitive awareness, you'll realize you don't need external validation—you already have the answers within.

Experience a transformative meditation that connects you to your Intuition—your personal knowing beyond egoic thoughts and beliefs. The meditation is in the workbook. Head over and enjoy!

> *"I never made one of my discoveries through the process of rational thinking."*
>
> *— Albert Einstein*
>
> Write without thinking. What shows up when your soul is speaking and your ego is silent?

CHAPTER 8

CLARITY PROCESS

Your personal power lives in one of two places: actively moving toward your desired end result, or getting caught in the cycle of resolving internal identity conflicts. When you're not moving forward, you're often looping in unresolved questions about who you believe yourself to be.

Problems are endless. And once you've proven you can solve them, your subconscious may continue generating more—just to keep proving it.

Solving problems may feel productive, but it rarely brings you closer to your heart's desires. Creation, not correction, is the path to fulfillment.

Your beliefs do not bind your creative spirit, and true power emerges through the act of choosing—a formalization of your will.

In this chapter, we will learn to recognize where you stand—whether in alignment with your desires or entangled in identity conflicts—then consciously choose the path forward.

When something feels uncertain, clarity comes by asking the right questions. You begin to uncover the inner conflict, identify the beliefs behind it, and then consciously decide what you want to believe instead.

That simple shift—deciding what to believe—empowers you to move forward.

You can decide to stay in victim mode. Or you can recognize your current pattern and consciously shift into the vision that calls your desires forward.

For instance, "I never get what I want" can shift to "I'm learning to ask for what I want with confidence."

While you may not yet be where you want to be, this process clears the path and gives you the empowerment necessary to align with your desires. It also brings awareness to where you're choosing to operate from.

By asking and answering key questions, you shift into the observer role. From there, you can choose where to focus.

Focusing on the issue itself keeps you stuck. It offers no pleasure, no power, and no path forward.

Instead, focus on what you desire. Observe your current state without judgment. Be honest. Be kind. Just notice where you are—and where you would rather be.

Think deeply about these questions in the workbook. Then write down whatever comes to mind.

Your inner truth will begin to speak. Your heart will guide you. And when your vision is rooted in love, wisdom appears.

Wisdom is the obvious next step—the action that feels clear and true.

Since energy follows the path of least resistance, your clarity aligns every part of your mind toward your desired outcome.

Final Thoughts:

Whatever you focus on becomes your reality.

So ask yourself with love and courage:

What am I choosing?

Where is the power?

Go to the workbook and do this short meditation prior to the worksheets for inspiration.

"Between stimulus and response, there is a space. In that space is our power to choose."

— *Viktor E. Frankl*

Conflict is not the problem. The unprocessed emotion is.

What if your biggest fight is with a belief, not a person?

CHAPTER 9

PUTTING IT ALL TOGETHER

Achieving clarity and a comprehensive understanding of all the modules, integrating their insights and practices into a cohesive and empowered approach to your life and goals, will bring about the results you desire.

Let's create a personalized schedule for practicing the meditations, which will provide fresh clarity and insights as you move forward. You'll establish a daily routine to align your choices with your goals. Discover how to use the Manifesting Tree to focus your energy effectively and learn the Completion exercise to free your subconscious from lingering tasks or unfulfilled desires, enabling you to step into your future with ease and purpose."

Knowing your operating system, making aligned choices, listening to your intuition, listening to your heart, integrating your shadow, clarifying where your power is and acknowledging that you have completed things are the operating procedures for getting your desired results.

Grab your coffee, tea, or lemon water first thing in the morning. Get your pen out and start writing two choices from your aligned choice list. Ask what you can do today to get these desires. Listen, follow, and act on the intuitive message you received. Feel what it feels like to have these desires. Write down the feelings. Visualize what you are doing when you have these desires. Write those down.

Focus on the desired reality. I like using the manifesting tree as a focusing tool on what it feels like to have my desire and what I am doing when I get to my desired result. I recommend really feeling it, everywhere in your body, where does it land in your body along with seeing what I am doing now that I have this. It is very powerful and keeps one inspired and empowered, knowing that you are following your heart's desires. This is what keeps me going. The knowing, the empowerment, that by listening and doing, there is a guaranteed manifestation of any desire, any end result.

It is that simple. Really. One can live in the worst conditions and eventually, by focusing, listening, and doing, end up where they desire.

COMPLETION:

When you complete something, write this down. Your mind needs to know it has completed the task so it no longer looks for solutions. This is important. The energies will be used for our next desires! Yes, there are always more desires as we learn to say yes to ourselves. We expand even more, into our beautiful souls! I summarize my completions that occur each month and look back on them at the end of the year. It will amaze you how much you have accomplished. Reinforce your beautiful, creative soul by acknowledging and realizing your accomplishments.

By now, you have completed the following:

1. Know your operating system, your egoic agenda and acknowledge it.

2. Heart-Guided Writing

    a.   Do quarterly at a minimum

3. Meet your Shadow and integrate.

4. Completed your Aligned Choices

    a.   Update with heart-guided writing quarterly

5. Align All Energies Within

6. How to utilize the Manifestation tree

7. How to tap into your Intuition

    a.   Practice daily

    b.   Write down the small wins daily

    c.   Write down the big wins daily

8. Understand the Completion Process. Write down what was completed. This can be anything; nothing is too small to acknowledge that it was completed.

9. Use the Self-Reflection exercise for anything that was uncomfortable the day before. This reinforces where your power is and acknowledges there was a moment where you were uncomfortable. It is important to acknowledge this so that your focus and energies can go towards your desires.

> **Say yes.**

10. Feel it, see it, be it.

11. Incorporate the Daily Vision Practice into your morning routine

> *"Success is neither magical nor mysterious. Success is the natural consequence of consistently applying the basic fundamentals."*
>
> *— Jim Rohn*
>
> What's one small daily practice that—if done consistently—would change everything?

THE SUCCESS ZONES WORKBOOK

Desire . Align . Manifest.

Before beginning the workbook, I recommend having a journal ready and using red ink pens. Different colors of ink have different effects on our brains. Using red will propel our desires, and that is our goal.

This workbook corresponds to a Chapter in the book. It contains the meditations and worksheets necessary to incorporate The Success Zones needed to manifest one's heart's desires and live with clarity, empowerment, and peace.

To find the meditations go to **https://www.thesuccesszones.com**

Color	Emotional & Brain Effect	Use It For
Red	Focus, urgency, passion, courage. Activates attention and recall.	Desires, power statements, declarations, emotional breakthroughs
Blue	Calming, clarity, openness. Enhances creativity and expansive thinking.	Dreams, visions, intuition, future self journaling
Green	Balance, growth, healing. Regulates the nervous system.	Heart-centered writing, gratitude, forgiveness, growth tracking

Yellow	Joy, motivation, clarity. Stimulates confidence and optimism.	Wins, confidence building, affirmations, success journaling
Purple	Intuition, higher self, wisdom. Inspires spiritual insight and reflection.	Channeling, heart-guided writing, purpose work
Orange	Creativity, emotional connection, pleasure. Awakens sensuality and flow.	Manifestation scripting, sensory writing, pleasure mapping
Black	Mystery, shadow, grounding. Anchors deep truths or subconscious material.	Shadow work, fears, limiting beliefs, truth-telling
White	Clarity, reset, cleansing. Feels like space and openness.	Reflection, new beginnings, clearing exercises

CHAPTER 1

YOUR MIND WORKSHEETS

Let's Put This Into Action:

Section 1: Awareness

1. Something I would like to accomplish is:

   _____

2. The first thought that came into my mind about why I can't do this is: _____

3. This message likely came from my (ego / subconscious / childhood belief): _____

4. A more empowering thought I could choose is:

   _____

5. When I believe the empowering thought, I feel:

   _____

Section 2: In-Depth Reflections

Reflect on the following prompts in your journal or the space below.

- What limiting belief came up when you thought of your goal?

- Where do you think that belief came from? Childhood? A specific event?

- What feelings arise when you think about that belief?

- What would you rather believe instead?

- How would you feel if you truly believed your new empowering thought?

- Where do you feel this new belief in your body? Describe it.

Section 3: Enneagram Type Discovery

Take the Enneagram Type Quiz from the workbook and record your results below.

Top Type: _____

Runner-Up Type: _____

Notes or Observations: _____

_____

Section 4: Ego Awareness Tracker

- What did your ego say today that made you doubt yourself?

- What is the real truth you want to believe instead?

- How will you respond to your ego next time this thought arises?

Section 5: Journal Prompt – What's Holding Me Back?

Write freely about your inner voice, your ego's messages, and the patterns you've observed.

Prompt: "Why do I believe I can't have what I desire, and what truth do I now choose instead?"

Enneagram Type Quiz

Part 1: Type Discovery Questions

1. Choose the statement that best describes you:

   A. I strive to do what is right and fair.

   B. I want to feel needed and appreciated.

   Your choice (A/B): _____

2. Choose the statement that best describes you:

   A. I value order and high standards.

   B. I enjoy helping and connecting with others.

   Your choice (A/B): _____

3. Choose the statement that best describes you:

   A. I can be critical when things are out of line.

   B. I tend to take on others' needs as my own.

   Your choice (A/B): _____

4. Choose the statement that best describes you:

   A. I pursue goals and want to be seen as successful.

   B. I am driven by a need to feel unique and special.

   Your choice (A/B): _____

5. Choose the statement that best describes you:

   A. I like to be efficient and productive.

   B. I spend time reflecting on deep emotions.

   Your choice (A/B): _____

6. Choose the statement that best describes you:

    A. I adapt to what others expect to win approval.

    B. I withdraw to protect my identity.

    Your choice (A/B): _____

7. Choose the statement that best describes you:

    A. I seek knowledge and independence.

    B. I want security and strong support.

    Your choice (A/B): _____

8. Choose the statement that best describes you:

    A. I value privacy and prefer minimal obligations.

    B. I tend to prepare for worst-case scenarios.

    Your choice (A/B): _____

9. Choose the statement that best describes you:

    A. I focus on ideas and concepts.

    B. I rely on trusted authorities or communities.

    Your choice (A/B): _____

10. Choose the statement that best describes you:

    A. I love options and new adventures.

    B. I prefer comfort and keeping the peace.

    Your choice (A/B): _____

11. Choose the statement that best describes you:

    A. I avoid pain and seek pleasure.

    B. I avoid conflict and go along with others.

    Your choice (A/B): _____

12. Choose the statement that best describes you:

    A. I get bored easily and like stimulation.

    B. I focus on harmony and stability.

    Your choice (A/B): _____

13. Choose the statement that best describes you:

    A. I take charge and challenge limitations.

    B. I feel emotions deeply and want authenticity.

    Your choice (A/B): _____

14. Choose the statement that best describes you:

    A. I don't mind confrontation if needed.

    B. I am sensitive and value meaningful experiences.

    Your choice (A/B): _____

15. Choose the statement that best describes you:

    A. I respect strength and directness.

    B. I often feel misunderstood or different.

    Your choice (A/B): _____

Scoring Your Results

Tally your A and B answers using the answer key below.

Each choice corresponds to one of the nine Enneagram types.

The two types you score highest in are likely your strongest operating types.

Top Type: _____

Runner Up: _____

Notes: _____

Answer Key

Question 1: A = Type 1, B = Type 2

Question 2: A = Type 1, B = Type 2

Question 3: A = Type 1, B = Type 2

Question 4: A = Type 3, B = Type 4

Question 5: A = Type 3, B = Type 4

Question 6: A = Type 3, B = Type 4

Question 7: A = Type 5, B = Type 6

Question 8: A = Type 5, B = Type 6

Question 9: A = Type 5, B = Type 6

Question 10: A = Type 7, B = Type 9

Question 11: A = Type 7, B = Type 9

Question 12: A = Type 7, B = Type 9

Question 13: A = Type 8, B = Type 4

Question 14: A = Type 8, B = Type 4

Question 15: A = Type 8, B = Type 4

TALLY YOUR TYPES

Enneagram Type	# of A or B Answers	Notes or Insights
Type 1		
Type 2		
Type 3		
Type 4		
Type 5		
Type 6		
Type 7		
Type 8		
Type 9		

CHAPTER 2

GOOD CHOICES VS. ALIGNED CHOICES WORKSHEETS

Experience an incredible meditation that guides you to your Field of Infinite Possibilities—a place where your greatest desires take form. Discover the gift waiting for you there and write down everything you find, describing it in vivid detail. This journey sparks the imagination, unveiling some of your greatest choices and allowing space for dreams you haven't yet acknowledged. Step into a world of limitless possibilities and bring your positive vision to life.

Use this visualization to enter a deeply imaginative and energetically open state. Let your hand write freely without judgment. This space is for exploring desires, dreams, and unexpected insights.

FIELD OF INFINITE POSSIBILITIES MEDITATION:

Settle into your chair now. Let the weight of the day begin to dissolve. With your pen in hand and your journal open in front of you, take a deep breath with me. I invite you to join me on this journey—not one of expectation, but of discovery. A journey into the Field of Infinite Possibilities.

Let's begin by simply noticing.

What has brought you to this moment?

What thoughts are drifting through your mind?

What emotions are stirring within you?

There's no need to change them—just allow them to be. Observe without judgment.

Now, gently close your eyes.

70

I want you to imagine that you are a blue mist—weightless, free, suspended above the earth. Feel the cool moisture of your form and the delicate swirling of your blue particles. Float effortlessly. Let yourself shift with the currents, moving in perfect harmony with the air around you.

Feel yourself being gently pulled—drawn toward the entrance of a vast tunnel carved into the heart of a great mountain. It's wide, welcoming, glowing with a soft, luminous light. Allow yourself to be guided forward into the tunnel. Drift deeper within, the walls around you shimmering as you glide through.

Now feel the tunnel begin to shift—it's no longer descending. It's climbing. You're ascending steadily. The movement picks up speed. The light becomes more brilliant. You begin to glow brighter—electric blue, pulsing with energy.

Faster and faster you move, until motion ceases. You are still, yet everywhere. Your light is so pure and radiant that you become transparent—empty, yet full. In this stillness, feel the expansion… the opening… and then—

You emerge.

You step into the Field of Infinite Possibilities.

As you shift gently back into your body, take in your surroundings. This is a place like no other. It is limitless. Abundant. It is created just for you. The air hums with potential. The sky stretches endlessly. Everything pulses with a quiet, knowing presence.

Now, notice what waits before you—a gift. Reach out and allow it to take form. Maybe it's an object. Maybe it's a feeling. Maybe it's an understanding you've long sought. Whatever it is, accept it. Hold it close. You don't need to know its meaning yet—just trust that it has purpose.

Now it's time to explore.

Begin walking the land. With each step, you uncover treasures—dreams, desires, truths you may have never dared to claim. As you

71

discover them, write them down. Let your pen move freely. Name what you find. No judgment, no limitations—only possibility.

Keep writing. Trust what shows up.

And now pause. Ask yourself gently: What else?

What remains unseen... unspoken... unclaimed?

What have you not yet allowed yourself to receive?

Open your mind. Open your heart. Let the answer emerge. Even if it surprises you. Especially if it surprises you. Welcome it fully.

And when you feel that you've gathered everything meant for you in this moment, take a slow, deep breath.

Know this: Your Field of Infinite Possibilities is always here. Its gifts are endless. You can return anytime.

When you're ready, open your eyes. Feel the journal in your hands. The words you've written are alive with potential. The journey may be complete for now—but its gifts remain.

And so, you step forward...

Carrying with you the abundance of your Field of Infinite Possibilities.

After you do the meditation, make a list of everything you can imagine you would like to have, to be, to do—no limitations. It doesn't matter if you have any ability or knowledge about how you would get it or go about it. That is **not** the exercise. Write it down! **Dream BIG!!!**

Section 1: Awareness

1. One choice I made recently that felt misaligned was:

   _____

2. I made that choice because: _____

3. A choice I made that felt aligned and true was:

   _____

4. The difference in how I felt between the two choices was:

   _____

5. Today, I choose to: _____
   (an aligned, heart-centered choice)

Section 2: In-Depth Reflections

- Make a list of everything you do NOT want. Then reflect: How often are your choices made to avoid these outcomes rather than to pursue your desires?

- What are some stories or limitations you've told yourself when considering a big dream or desire?

- What does it feel like in your body when you are making an aligned choice? What signals or sensations arise?

- How do you imagine your superconscious responds when you say 'yes' to your desires?

Section 3: Field of Infinite Possibilities

After completing the meditation, use the space below to describe your vision.

- What did you receive in the Field? (object, gift, feeling, understanding?)

- What did you discover about what you truly desire?

- How will you honor these desires moving forward?

Section 4: Aligned Choices & Goal Tracker

List 13 goals that reflect your aligned desires. Begin with the four non-negotiable ones listed in the book:

1. I choose a Life I Love

2. I choose Health and Vitality

3. I choose to Live My True Nature and Purpose

4. I choose to Be the Primary Creative Force in My Life

5. _____

6. _____

7. _____

8. _____

9. _____

10. _____

11. _____

12. _____

13. _____

Next to each one, note where you are in the process—just beginning, taking action, halfway there, or completed.

Section 5: Journal Prompt – Yes to Me!

Write freely about what saying 'yes' to yourself looks and feels like.

Prompt: "If I fully trusted that everything I desire is on its way, what would I choose today?"

CHAPTER 3

HEART -GUIDED WRITING WORKSHEETS

JOURNEY TO YOUR HEART MEDITATION

Close your eyes. Breathe.

Begin by settling in. Let your body relax and soften. Take a slow, deep breath with me… and exhale. Feel the weight of the world begin to fall away.

Now, let your imagination open.

The forest path is soft beneath your feet. With each step, you feel the give of earth beneath you, and the scent of damp soil rises gently in the air. You breathe in deeply, allowing the air to fill your lungs—and as you exhale, feel yourself releasing tension you didn't even realize you were holding. Each breath comes easily. Naturally. There is nothing you need to do now except walk, observe, and simply be.

As you move down the winding trail, the towering trees around you sway gently in the breeze. Their branches whisper, but not with words—with something only your heart can hear. You listen—not just with your ears, but with your whole being. Each step draws you deeper into the woods… and deeper into yourself.

Ahead, the path forks. No signs. No directions. And yet—you know. Instinctively, you feel which way is yours. The left path calls to you—not in sound, but in silent knowing.

So you follow.

As you walk, your senses heighten. You smell the rich pine in the air… hear the crunch of twigs beneath your steps… feel the soft caress of wind on your skin. Your mind is quiet now. Still. Then, just ahead, the trees begin to part.

A clearing opens before you, bathed in golden light.

All around, violet flowers stretch endlessly across the field. Their delicate petals shimmer as if lit from within, swaying as if welcoming you. You step forward slowly, letting your hands graze the tops of the blossoms. They feel familiar somehow—like a memory you didn't know you lost.

And then, in the distance—you see it.

A building.

Grand, yet simple. Ancient, yet timeless. You don't question it. You don't hesitate. You move toward it, as if guided by something greater than logic—a deeper pull from within.

With every step closer, the energy around the building begins to hum. You can feel it vibrate through the air itself. When you reach the entrance, a great portal stands before you. As you approach, it opens—not with sound, but with welcome.

Step inside.

The air shifts. You're inside a vast interior, lined with soaring halls and endless corridors. The walls around you seem alive—alive with knowledge. They speak to you, not with words, but with a wisdom you've always known but never learned.

Allow your curiosity to lead you forward.

Down a long hallway, you see it: a single crib. And inside, a baby lies peacefully—eyes wide with wonder.

This is not just any child.

This is you. Or rather, the essence of you. Before the world shaped you. Before the layers. Before the beliefs. Before the expectations.

You walk closer. You kneel beside the crib. The baby looks at you—not with judgment or fear. Only pure awareness. Pure observation.

Then you know what to do.

You become the baby.

Now, you are looking up at the world with unfiltered awe. Every color, every shape, every sound is new. There is no past. No future. Only now.

Suddenly, the ground beneath you opens. And you begin to fall.

Gently. Weightlessly. Like a feather floating downward.

Above you, the sky stretches into forever, glittering with stars. But these stars are more than light. They are your thoughts... beliefs... the stories you've told yourself about who you are.

And as you fall, those stars begin to drift away. Dissolving. You are letting them go.

You are free now. Free from assumptions. Free from identities. Free from everything you thought you had to be.

You are falling into your essence—your truth—pure, limitless, and untouched by expectation.

A violet void surrounds you now, wrapping you in deep, musical silence. You are nothing... and yet, everything.

And then, a shift.

The motion begins to slow.

You feel yourself returning. Gently. Softly. You are not falling anymore—you're floating downward... drifting back into your body.

Your eyes remain closed. But you feel it.

You are here. You are now. And you are changed.

When you're ready, slowly open your eyes. Let them land on something nearby—a plant... a book... a ray of light through the window.

Look at it. Really see it. As if for the first time.

Because in a way... You are.

The world around you hasn't changed. But you have.

You have returned—but not as you were.

You've remembered the truth that was always there.

And now... you know.

You have always known.

Section 1: Awareness

1. When I tune into my heart, I feel:

    _____

2. A desire that consistently arises from my heart is:

    _____

3. One way I can act on this desire today is:

    _____

4. When I write from my heart, I notice:

    _____

5. My heart wants me to know:

    _____

Section 2: In-Depth Reflections

- What's the difference between writing from the head vs. writing from the heart?

- What signals does your heart give you when something is aligned?

- How do you feel when your heart is silenced or ignored?

- What is your heart asking you to pay attention to right now?

- How would your life change if you made all your choices from your heart's truth?

Section 3: Journey to Your Heart Meditation Reflection

After reading, listening, or recording the 'Journey to Knowing' meditation, reflect on these questions:

- What parts of the journey resonated most with you?

- What was revealed in the vision or memory?

- What message did your heart or your inner child have for you?

Section 4: Heart-Guided Writing Prompts

Use red or purple ink to activate focus and heart wisdom. Set a timer for 10–15 minutes and allow your writing to flow freely.

Prompt 1: "Dear Heart, what do you want me to know right now?"

Prompt 2: "What would you have me choose today?"

Prompt 3: "If I truly trusted myself, what would I do?"

Section 5: Integration Notes

Use this page to note any recurring patterns, powerful statements, or new awareness that came through during your writing.

_____

_____

_____

_____

_____

CHAPTER 4

YOUR SHADOW WORKSHEETS

Have a pen and paper ready and within your reach.

Close your eyes after reading sentences and really choose to meet your shadow side and receive the information that needs to be shared. Just choose this for a moment. Close your eyes, settle in, and notice your body and breath. Just take this moment, let go of everything, disconnect, and go into your body. Becoming aware of the flow of your breath, in and out of your body; breathing in, breathing out. There's nothing you need to do right now; everything is perfect the way it is. Just notice your body and your breath. That's it.

THE POND OF SHADOWS MEDITATION

Walk with me now, along a forest path. Feel the earth steady beneath your feet. The trees stretch high above, their branches swaying gently, whispering to one another. Sunlight filters through the leaves, dappling the forest floor in warm, golden patches. Breathe in deeply—wood, earth, and something faintly sweet fill your lungs. This forest is alive, holding you, watching, waiting.

There is no destination, yet you are being guided. Let your steps be easy, unhurried. This is a place of peace—allow it to hold you.

Ahead, the path splits. One trail continues straight, familiar and open. The other bends left, disappearing into the deeper part of the forest. Feel the gentle pull—a quiet, insistent force—guiding you toward the left. Follow it.

As you walk deeper, the world grows quieter. The air thickens, not with weight, but with presence. Shadows stretch across the ground. You feel not fear, but anticipation.

And then, the trees' part. A clearing opens before you. You arrive and take in the beautiful scene—smooth stones, soft grass, blooming flowers, and in the center, a still, dark pond.

There is something sacred here, something ancient.

Step forward, drawn to the pond's edge. You sit beside it, knowing something important is about to happen.

The water moves. Ripples spread, forming shifting patterns. A shape begins to rise—at first a mist, then a form. Recognition dawns. It is you, not your reflection, but something deeper. A presence that has always been there. A being. A symbol. Your shadow side. Your shadow. Hold your ground. Stay steady. Ask it gently, 'Who are you?' It comes closer. You meet it. Heart to heart. You know this moment matters.

Ask your shadow to share what you need to understand. What you need to acknowledge. What must be released. Ask your shadow for all the relevant information. Ask again, 'Why are you here?' It speaks without sound—of pain you've silenced, anger denied, fears hidden. Of truths unspoken, desires left unfulfilled, of moments when you abandoned yourself. Listen. Feel the recognition settle—not as a burden, but as truth. These are not strangers. These are parts of you.

Now, pick up your journal. Your pen. And begin to write. Write the truths you've feared to face. The wounds. The anger. The longings. Let it all spill out. Unfiltered. Unedited. Keep writing until there is nothing left unspoken. When you are done, pause. Breathe. Feel the space that has opened inside you.

Look up. The shadow watches. This time, you meet its gaze. And you do not flinch. Whisper: 'Thank you. Watch it nod. And like mist in the morning sun—it fades. The pond stills. The forest breathes. Something inside you has shifted. Your shadow has not left—it has come home. It is no longer something to fear. It is something to understand. Rise. Return to the path. Your steps are lighter. Your breath is deeper. You walk forward—not in fear of your shadow, but with the knowledge that it, too, is part of your light.

Let the truth flow. Keep writing until you are complete.

Section 1: Awareness

1. One part of myself I often try to hide or suppress is:

   _____

2. This part of me shows up when:

   _____

3. I often feel _____ when this part surfaces. (e.g., ashamed, afraid, angry)

4. If I could say one kind thing to this part of me, it would be:

   _____

5. A situation where I recently judged someone else harshly was: _____

6. That judgment might be pointing to a hidden part of me that: _____

Section 2: In-Depth Reflections

- What triggers or patterns keep repeating in your life, and what do they reveal about unacknowledged parts of yourself?

- What feelings do you find most uncomfortable to feel or express?

- What qualities in others do you most criticize or envy?

- What parts of your childhood shaped what you see as 'bad' or unacceptable in yourself?

- How would your life change if you accepted these parts instead of rejecting them?

Section 3: The Pond of Shadows Meditation Reflection

After listening to or reading the meditation, answer the following:

- What did your shadow side look or feel like in the vision?

- What did it say or reveal to you?

- What emotions came up as you met this part of yourself?

- What message did your shadow want you to hear and understand?

Section 4: Letter from the Shadow / Letter to the Shadow

Take time to write a letter "from" your shadow to you. Let it speak freely. Then respond with a letter "to" your shadow from your current self.

This is a powerful way to build trust and integration between your conscious and unconscious selves.

Section 5: Journal Prompt – Embracing All of Me

Prompt: "What parts of myself have I been afraid to face, and what do I now see clearly about their purpose in my life?"

CHAPTER 5

ALIGN ALL ENERGIES WITHIN WORKSHEETS

Let's do this meditation first, then fill out the worksheets.

A Journey Through Past, Present, and Future

Go ahead and close your eyes. Take a deep, slow breath in… and out.

Let yourself settle into comfort as you prepare to align with your highest vision. This moment is just for you—to connect with your emotions, your energy, and your future.

First, I want you to bring up a clear image of where you are right now in your life.

What's happening in your world? What do you have? What are you creating? And how do you feel?

Now shift your focus just a few steps forward to a goal you deeply desire.

See it clearly. Feel how much you want it.

As you feel that desire, notice how you feel right now. There's a space between where you are and where you want to be—and that's okay. Allow yourself to feel it fully.

Now take a gentle step backward in your mind. Remember who you were just before you got to where you are today.

That version of you made brave decisions, took action, and made it through hard times. Maybe you changed jobs, started something new, let go of something heavy, or made a bold choice.

Take a moment to thank that version of you. They helped you get here.

Back then, you dreamed of being where you are now—and you made it happen.

Feel the appreciation for how far you've come. Even if you're not exactly where you want to be yet, acknowledge that you've already grown, already changed, already succeeded. Breathe in deep gratitude for that.

Now, gently shift your attention toward your next step forward.

What is the first step toward that big goal? You don't need to know every step—just the next one.

See it in your mind. Maybe it's a habit you want to build, a decision you need to make, a conversation you're ready to have, or a belief you're ready to shift.

Whatever it is, see yourself stepping into that next move. Let yourself feel how it would feel to already be there.

What would you say to yourself if it was already done? What would you believe about yourself? About life?

Breathe that feeling into your body.

Now step forward again, to the next milestone. See yourself there.

Maybe you've created something new, embodied a new mindset, or taken aligned action.

Let the past version of you fall away. Thank them—they carried you here.

How does it feel to have made it this far? What do you see around you? How do you stand, walk, and breathe?

Let yourself feel proud. Let yourself feel that this is real.

Now see the final step before your desired goal. You are only one step away.

Smile—because you know you've come this far, and you can go further.

And when you're ready, take that final step. Step into the version of you who has already achieved the goal.

Feel it in your body. How do you move, speak, and show up now that you've made it?

Let yourself celebrate this moment.

Remember the path that brought you here. Know it couldn't have happened any other way. Even the detours were guiding you.

Feel gratitude for every version of you—the one in the past, the one today, and the one you are becoming.

Thank yourself for continuing. For choosing. For believing.

Now that you've reached this goal, ask yourself: Where am I going next?

A word, image, or feeling may come. Whatever it is, step into that new vision in your mind.

Walk past this goal and into a future that is still unfolding. Feel the energy pulling you forward, like a magnet.

That future version of you is calling you forward—with love, with pride. They are cheering you on.

Now gently return to the present moment. Come back to today.

Take a breath and ask yourself: What is the one step I will take today to move forward?

Breathe into that step. Feel it. See it. Commit to it.

And remember—there's a version of you in the future who is so grateful you didn't give up. So proud that you listened. That you took the next step. That you became who you came here to be.

Whenever you're ready, open your eyes. And carry that feeling with you—aligned, grateful, and ready.

Grab your journal and take a deep breath. Let's explore what's beneath the surface.

Section 1: Awareness

1. One recent situation where I felt out of alignment was:

2. I noticed these thoughts during that time:

3. The emotion(s) I felt were:

4. My ego wanted me to believe:

5. My subconscious patterns showed up as:

6. A more aligned thought I choose now is:

Section 2: In-Depth Reflections

- What does alignment feel like in your body, thoughts, and actions?

- How can you recognize when you are misaligned (with your thoughts, energy, or behaviors)?

- What part of your mind usually takes over when you're out of alignment (ego, subconscious, unconscious)?

- How does your superconscious guide you back into alignment?

- What practices help you shift back into focus when you get derailed?

Section 3: Reclaiming Your Power – Self-Reflection

- What situation in your life feels difficult right now?

- What emotions and thoughts come up with it?

- Revisit a childhood memory where a similar emotion first appeared.

- What beliefs were created then?

- How are they still affecting you?

- What strength or gift came from that time?

- How can you use that strength now?

Section 4: Alignment Meditation Reflection

After completing the Alignment Meditation, reflect:

- What version of yourself are you stepping into?

- What old version are you thanking and releasing?

- What is one inspired step you can take today to reinforce your alignment?

Section 5: Journal Prompt – Shifting Into Alignment

Prompt: "What would it look like to have all parts of my mind working in harmony with my desires?"

A. Identify the Challenge

- What situation in your life feels difficult right now, or what recent experience has been on your mind?

- What thoughts are circling this issue?

- What emotions come up when you think about it?

- How does this situation affect the way you see yourself?

- How does it shape your relationships with others?

- If you zoom out and look at the bigger picture, how does it connect to the world around you?

B. Revisit a Moment in Childhood

- Close your eyes and let your mind drift to a moment in your early years. What age comes to mind first? Trust the number that arises.

- What was life like for you at that time?

- What beliefs or decisions were you forming about yourself, others, and the world?

- What insights come to you as you reflect on this?

C. Unearthing Your Power

- Where did your personal power reside at that age?

- What did you give importance to?

- How much energy did you invest in that belief or focus?

- What was the outcome of this fixation or belief?

- Who were the key figures influencing this experience?

D. Shifting Perspective with Gratitude

- Every person and every experience—whether positive or challenging—has played a role in shaping you. Take a moment to express gratitude to all who were present in your early life and, most importantly, to yourself.

E. A New Perspective on the Present

- With this fresh awareness, how do you now view the problem you originally wrote about?

- What new wisdom or strength can you bring to it?

- How do you reclaim your power in this situation?

Final Thought:

Acknowledge the resilience, wisdom, and brilliance that have always been within you. Your awareness and perspective have the power to shift your experience.

Where's the power?

This exercise helps you see where the power is and choose which path to take. You can look at current issues objectively and then use your intuition to move through them. This is in total alignment with how your mind works with your heart.

Do this exercise whenever you need to change your focus, whenever you need to re-group, whenever you need help remembering where your power lies!

It is a wonderful place to learn how to refocus and take inspired action on our aligned desires and goals. It is empowering and comforting.

CHAPTER 6

MANIFESTATION WORKSHEETS

Do this meditation and then fill out the following worksheet.

A Journey to Reinforce My Goal, Belief, and Way of Being

Before we begin, make sure you have your goal, your new belief, how you want to feel, and how you want to be—written down in front of you.

Take a deep breath in... and out. As you look down at what you've written, breathe with intention.

Now write down three emotions you'll feel when this goal is true for you. You may write more if you'd like.

Examples:

If your goal is to be a millionaire, you might feel abundant, joyful, and free.

If your belief is that you're fully confident, you might feel proud, powerful, and excited.

Write down your own three feelings now. If you need to pause and do this, now is the time.

Next, write down three things that will be different about your life when you fully believe and live this truth.

Examples:

If you're a millionaire, maybe you'll drive your dream car, live in your ideal home, and travel the world.

If you're confident, maybe you'll speak on stage, enjoy a healthy relationship, and welcome more success.

Write down your own three changes now—what will be different when this is real. Pause if you need to.

Now, let's begin.

Close your eyes. Breathe in through your nose… and out through your mouth. Let yourself relax.

Starting at the top of your head, let a wave of relaxation move through you.

Relax your forehead… your eyebrows… the space around your eyes. Relax your cheeks, your jaw, and your lips.

Breathe again. As you exhale, soften your shoulders. Let the weight lift. Relax your arms, your chest, your upper back.

Let your breath fill your lungs easily. Feel the support of the seat beneath you.

Continue relaxing down through your hips, thighs, knees, calves… all the way to your feet and toes.

Your whole body is now calm, present, and still.

Take another deep breath in… and out.

Now, in your mind's eye, see a staircase in front of you, leading downward into peaceful darkness. There are 10 steps.

Take the first step… and relax deeper. Step 9… step 8… each step down brings more calm.

Step 7… 6… 5… even deeper now. Step 4… 3… your body feels heavy and light all at once.

Step 2… step 1… and finally, step 0.

You find yourself in a beautiful natural setting. You hear a stream in the distance, birds singing, maybe a breeze. The sun shines gently. You feel grounded in this sacred space.

Now, look up. In front of you is a large outdoor movie screen.

A movie begins to play—a movie of you, fully living your goal, embodying your belief, and being your highest self.

Watch yourself in this movie. See the three things that are different about your life. Watch how you move, speak, and show up.

See your posture, your presence, your power. Notice who's with you, what you're doing, and how it feels.

Let that good feeling rise inside you. Feel the desire to live this fully, not someday, but now.

Beside you, a remote control appears. On it is a big red button labeled NOW.

Look at that button. Ask yourself: Am I ready to become this version of me? Am I ready to release the old version behind me?

If the answer is yes, if you feel that desire, press the button.

Zoom. You're inside the movie now. No longer watching. You're living it.

Feel the shift. Feel the emotions you wrote earlier—confidence, abundance, joy, whatever you choose.

Amplify those feelings. Move your body like someone who lives this reality. Smile. Stand tall. Own it.

Turn the emotions up. From 1... to 2... to 3... let them grow stronger with each breath.

Feel it in your chest, your stomach, your hands, your heart.

Ask yourself: What do I need to release to turn it up more? What could someone say to help it grow?

Keep turning it up—4... 5... 6... let the feeling snowball. The more you feel it, the more real it becomes.

Now turn it up—7... 8... 9... and finally... 10. Let it vibrate through your whole being.

You are this person now. This is not a future you—it's who you are right now.

Breathe. Sit in this feeling. Memorize it. Teach your body how it feels.

This is who you are.

Now, look ahead. What's your next goal now that you've reached this one? Let a new vision arise. Step toward it.

The version of you who just reached this goal is already in your past. You're already on the path to something more.

Feel gratitude—for who you were, who you are, and who you're becoming.

Now, gently return to the present moment. Ask yourself: What's one small action I can take today to live as this version of me?

Commit to it now.

And when you're ready, open your eyes... to a new you. A new day. A new future.

Section 1: Awareness

1. One desire I want to manifest is:

   _____

2. The reason I want this is because:

   _____

3. My ego tries to block this desire by telling me:

   _____

4. My new belief to replace that block is:

_____

5. I will feel _____ when this desire
becomes real.

6. A small step I can take today toward this desire is:

_____

Section 2: In-Depth Reflections

- What has stopped you from manifesting this desire in the
past?

- What are your ego's objections and protective patterns
around this desire?

- What emotions and visuals come up when you imagine
already having it?

- Which Enneagram patterns might interfere with your
manifestation process?

- How does aligning your mind (conscious, subconscious,
unconscious) support your manifestation?

Section 3: 15-Minute Daily Manifestation Practice

1. Choose two desires:
   - Desire 1: _____
   - Desire 2: _____

2. Ask: "What action can I take today to get closer to these?"
   - Action: _____

3. Visualize each desire as already real. What do you feel?

4. What are you doing now that it's real?

5. Write the actions you are taking in that vision.

Section 4: Journal Prompt – Aligned Creation

Prompt: "What would change in my life if I truly believed I could have everything I desire?"

Section 5: Enneagram Type Awareness for Manifestation

Reflect on your Enneagram type and its common manifestation blocks. Then answer:

- What egoic agenda is trying to run the show?

- What shift can I make to stay in alignment?

- How can I use my type's gifts to manifest with more ease?

CHAPTER 7

INTUITION WORKSHEETS

Tuning In: A Morning Meditation for Intuitive Action

This short morning meditation is designed to help you tun into the wisdom of your inner guidance, so you can take aligned action today toward the goals that master most to you.

Gently close your eyes.

Sit upright, comfortably grounded. Take a slow breath in through your nose... and a full breath out through your mouth. Do this again, and feel your body begin to settle.

As you continue to breathe slowly, begin to scan your body. Notice any tension—maybe in your shoulders, jaw, or back—and invite those muscles to relax. Simply set the intention to release. Just by intending it, you begin to soften.

With each breath, allow your body to become more open... more ready to receive.

Now, bring your full attention to your breath. In through your nose... and out through your mouth. You don't need to change anything. Just observe.

Become aware of this natural rhythm, and allow it to anchor you into the present moment.

Now, place your attention on your heart—the center of your being.

You might place a hand there or gently sense into it. Feel the stillness, the wisdom. Let your breath move through you as you connect with the quiet knowing that lives in your heart.

This is the part of you that sees clearly. That isn't confused or rushed. That always knows the next right step.

Now, gently turn your attention to the day ahead.

Ask yourself—softly, sincerely: What is one aligned action I can take today that will move me toward my goal?

What would feel natural, easeful, and powerful?

What does your inner wisdom want you to do today to move forward?

Remind yourself you're working on just two goals. That focus brings clarity. You don't need to figure out the whole path—you just need today's action.

Stay open to receive. Maybe it's a word, a phrase, a feeling, or an image. Trust what comes. Your intuition speaks in many ways, and you are listening.

Breathe in this guidance. Let it settle within you.

When you're ready, open your eyes and write down the action you received.

This is your aligned step for today. You don't need to know how it all unfolds. Just follow the nudge, take the step, and trust the process.

Carry this clarity with you into your day.

And so, it begins.

Section 1: Awareness

1. A time I wish I had trusted my intuition was:

   _____

2. My body usually tells me something is off by:

   _____

3. When something is in alignment, I feel:

_____

4. One way I can strengthen my intuition is:

_____

5. My intuition often speaks to me through:

_____

6. Today, my intuition is nudging me to:

_____

Section 2: In-Depth Reflections

- How has ignoring your intuition affected your past decisions or outcomes?

- What's your relationship with stillness and listening inwardly?

- Where do fear or logic tend to override your intuitive guidance?

- What is one consistent pattern you notice when your intuition is correct?

- How can you better integrate your intuition into your daily routine?

Section 3: Morning Intuition Practice

1. Sit quietly and breathe deeply.

2. Ask yourself: "What is one aligned action I can take today toward my goals?"

3. Write down what you hear, feel, or see:

_____

4. What two goals are you focusing on today?

   - Goal 1: _____

   - Goal 2: _____

5. How does your body respond to the intuitive guidance?

Section 4: Journal Prompt – Listening Inward

Prompt: "What is my intuition asking me to do, be, or become right now?"

Section 5: Intuition Development Log

Track your intuitive hits this week:

- Intuition I received: _____

- What I did with it: _____

- Outcome: _____

- Lesson learned:

Repeat this each day to build confidence and clarity in your inner guidance.

CHAPTER 8

CLARITY WORKSHEETS

3-Minute Daily Meditation: Set My Intention

I close my eyes and sit upright, letting myself get comfortable.

I take a deep breath in through my nose... and slowly exhale through my mouth.

Again, I breathe in... and out.

As I keep breathing deeply, I gently scan my body.

I notice where I feel any tightness.

I don't need to fix it—just set the intention to let it go.

I allow my body to soften, release, and relax.

If I need to shift my position, I do that now.

Now I bring my attention to my breath.

I feel the air moving in through my nose... and out through my mouth.

There's nothing I need to do—just observe.

This moment is just for me. I feel myself breathing, and I simply notice how it feels.

Now, I gently bring my focus to the center of my chest—my heart.

I can place my hand there if I want to.

I feel into this space.

I notice whatever is there, without needing to change it.

I am present—with my body, with my breath, and with my heart.

There's nothing to fix. Nothing to figure out.

Just this moment. Just me.

Now, I think about the day ahead.

I ask myself:

What is my intention for today?

Who do I want to be?

What do I want to feel, create, or focus on?

I pause. I listen.

I allow the answers to rise up from my heart, my inner wisdom, my calm knowing.

And when I feel ready, I open my eyes.

I take a moment to write down my intention for today.

This is my day. I choose how I want to live it.

Questions to activate, inspire, and assist with clarity:

Clarity Process

Section 1: Awareness

1. One area in my life where I feel unclear is:

   _____

2. The conflict I sense within myself around this is:

   _____

3. My current belief about this issue is:

   _____

4. The truth I would love to believe instead is:

   _____

5. If I had clarity right now, I would:

   _____

Section 2: In-Depth Reflections

- What internal conflict do you experience most often?
- What part of your identity feels most threatened when pursuing your desire?
- Are you choosing the problem or the solution? Why?
- How does choosing clarity feel different from problem-solving?
- What wisdom does your heart have about this situation?

Section 3: Clarity Worksheet

1. What is happening in your life right now?
2. What are you feeling?
3. What will resolve your discomfort or pain?
4. What is the loving way to deal with this?
5. What would you tell someone else in this situation?

6. What would you rather have or be?

7. What action can you take today to move toward that reality?

8. Which option has more power: your current focus or your desired vision?

9. Where will you choose to place your energy?

Section 4: Journal Prompt – Choosing Power Over Conflict

Prompt: "Where am I giving my power away through identity conflict, and how can I reclaim it?"

Section 5: Clarity Process Meditation Reflection

Reflect on the short clarity meditation:

- What feelings or images came up?
- Did a clear action or message emerge?
- What did you understand more clearly about your current position?

- How did you resolve all of the above?

- Where is the power?

CLARITY WORKSHEET

Use this worksheet to gain clarity, accept where you are, and know where you are going. There may not be enough room here, so use a journal and answer the following questions.

1. Describe what your reality is right now:

2. What are you feeling?

3. What will resolve your pain?

4. What is the loving way to deal with this? What would you tell someone else about how to deal with this?

5. What would you rather have? be?

6. What feelings does this bring in/up?

7. What action can you take today to have what you desire?

8. Which has more power?

Now, choose which position you would rather put your energy towards. This doesn't mean that the current reality will change this second. Just the way you see it and feel about it changes. Changing the focus to where the power is, is what is required here. It is important to be able to sit with where you are and focus on where you would rather be. That is part of the secret sauce!

CHAPTER 9

PUTTING IT ALL TOGETHER WORKSHEETS

Using the Daily Vision Practice, focuses you, your mind, and your soul on your Aligned Choices. This exercise does not take a lot of time and sets you up for success.

Daily Vision Practice

- Use the Daily Vision Practice worksheet and answer all the prompts.

- Then use the Manifesting trees and write your chosen aligned choice in the center of your tree. On the roots, note the feelings associated with having this. Be as concise with the feelings, using one feeling per root. Then, on the leaves describe what you are doing now that you have achieved the aligned choice.

Let's schedule doing this Daily Vision practice for when you wake up. I don't know if you drink coffee or tea or hot water, perhaps enjoy it while doing your Daily Vision practice. Doing the Daily Vision Practice first thing in the morning guides you throughout your day, inspires you and clears up issues from yesterday. It gives you the opportunity to tap into your intuition If you need clarity, do the clarity worksheet.

Schedule your heart-based writing twice a month or at least once a month. Staying in communication with yourself keeps you focused and aligned.

Checking in with yourself daily doesn't take much time, and the results are the fulfillment of your desires.

FEELINGS CHECKLIST

High-Energy/Positive		Neutral/Flat	
Energized & Activated		Bored	
Excited		Indifferent	
Energetic		Disconnected	
Enthusiastic		Numb	
Motivated		Apathetic	
Passionate		Meh	
Strong		Flat	
Adventurous		Uncertain	
Heart-Centered & Loving		Confused	
Loved		Waiting	
Connected		**Low-Energy/Difficult**	
Compassion		Activated but painful	
Grateful		Anger	
Appreciative		Critical	
Open-hearted		Righteous	
Empowered & Confident		Resentment	
Confident		Jealousy	
Proud		Hatred	
Trusting		Betrayed	
Knowing		Rejected	
Empowered		Threatened	
Worthy		**Emotional Pain/Hurt**	
Bliss	Hurt	Powerlessness/lack/fear	
Radiant	Disappointment	Trapped	
Clear	Lonely	Poor	
Clear	Grief	Cursed	
	Empty	Unlucky	
	Disconnected	Sinful	
	Unworthy		

DAILY VISION PRACTICE

My Aligned Choices (no more than 13):

1. Health and vitality

2. Financial Abundance

3. Life I love

4. Primary creative force in my life

5.

6.

7.

8.

9.

10.

11.

12.

13.

Today I am focused on (pick two from the list):

Use the Manifestation trees and fill in how you would feel if you achieved this now? And what will you be doing once you have achieved this aligned choice

Today I am grateful for:

_____

_____

_____

Other tasks I get to do today (priorities):

_____

_____

_____

Yesterday I felt frustration/negativity about (use Clarity worksheet if needed):

_____

_____

_____

Today my intuition tells me to do these actions:

_____

_____

_____

Ideas:

_____

_____

_____

I completed:

_____

_____

_____

PUTTING IT ALL TOGETHER

The following questions are also used once a month. These questions bring awareness and proof to yourself that you are on track.

Section 1: Awareness

1. My top 3 aligned desires are:

   _____

   _____

   _____

2. One powerful shift I've made in the past 8 weeks is:

   _____

3. A meditation or tool that worked really well for me was:

   _____

4. The most valuable thing I learned about myself is:

   _____

5. The next step I'm excited to take is:

   _____

Section 2: Integration Reflections

- How have your thoughts, emotions, and actions changed since beginning this journey?
- Which parts of your mind do you now notice more clearly in your day-to-day life?
- What does alignment look and feel like for you now?
- How do you now respond to fear, ego, or resistance when it shows up?
- What practice will you carry forward consistently?

Section 3: Completion Practice

This exercise helps your subconscious recognize when a desire or task is complete, allowing space for new creation.

1. What did you complete this week?

   - _____

2. What did you complete this month?

   - _____

3. What completion brought you the most satisfaction?

   - _____

4. How do you feel when you acknowledge your completions?

   - _____

5. How will you celebrate or mark this completion?

   - _____

Section 4: Journal Prompt – A New Chapter Begins

Prompt: "Now that I've completed this part of the journey, who am I becoming—and how will I continue to live in alignment with my desires?"